M000114465

Copyright © 2013 Rain Cameron, Deborah Grace, Kristin Rizzieri

You MAY reproduce this book in part, quote away, just give us credit. We'd be honored. If you want to use more than a page or two, contact us at www.weareviolet.com.

Cover kudos: Dorje Media, Misha Cherniske, Gemma Cross, Karina Cherniske

Published by Goldi Press

ISBN 978-0615852843

Printed in the United States of America

*To Music, the muse that connects us to our essence,
one another and Source*

Table of Contents

Violet the Band

*How Three Everyday Women
Rocked Everything*

Introduction

Please join us on a grand adventure, three women who wanted to have a group, not merely be groupies, who were tired of saying, "Perhaps someday I'll learn an instrument, be in a band." Women in the thick of mid-life (at the time of this writing our ages range from thirty-nine to fifty), in the thick of mothering (our combined ten children are three to twenty-years-old), we who are music lovers, yes, but not musicians.

This memoir, reflecting our collective and individual experiences, is told in three voices. Some of the writing pieces showcase our unique perspectives - for example, a concert we all attended and reviewed - while many events were original to each woman. We included details about our personal lives so that readers can see how music and creativity touched us as mothers, friends, partners and community members. What is gathered in these pages reflects our two-year journey on what we thought was just an attempt to play music together, but became much, much more. It is roughly chronological, beginning in the spring of 2010 and culminating in the summer of 2012.

Along the way, we gave ourselves permission to gather inspiration everywhere: in taking pictures to document our musical journey, we fell in love with photography; in wanting visual representation, we began collaging; not able to sit still when researching music, we sought out various forms of dance; inspired by others' creative lives, we began formally inter-viewing artists and musicians. From revamping our fashion to orchestrating birthday parties for our children, to navigating depression, everything became touched by our Violet experience.

We found others were touched as well. When out and about, the first question we three are asked is, "How is the band?" We hope this memoir serves to answer, and provides the impetus for everyone to move doggedly, divinely toward their dreams.

BALLAD OF THE BAND
BY RAIN

One starry night in March of 2010, my dear friend Deborah and I were trolling the streets of our town, Olympia, Washington, at this point in the evening feeling no pain. My stilettos were catching in every other treacherous sidewalk crack when I felt a sudden jolt of inspiration (or perhaps it was my heel). Said I, "I'm going to form a band called... Skanty Knickers! I've wanted to be in one all my life, and I just ran out of excuses not to. It will be my coping mechanism. Get divorced after twenty years of marriage, start a band. It's completely logical, really. Hiccup."

"What are you going to play?" asked the wide-eyed Deborah, whose heels weren't catching because she was sensibly wearing flats with her maxi-dress, her curls framing elfin goddess features.

"Drums!" I replied, surprising myself. What else *could* I play? Piano and violin teachers over the years had despaired of ever teaching me to read music. No matter how hard I tried, musical notes looked like nothing more than squished ants to me.

Deborah, as always, didn't miss a beat. "I'll be your lead singer. That's been my dream for forever, too." Could she sing? I soon found out, could she ever!

A week later, I told my flower-child friend, Kristin, as she was stripping down in my bedroom, raiding my closet for an upcoming wedding. The idea still looked good in the now-sober daylight. As scary as the thought was, it was secretly a relief to get it out in the open. Me. Band. Musician. Grunt. It was a primal urge, long stuffed in the overflowing back drawer labelled *who I would be if I only had the nerve*. I figured all I had to lose was my dignity and a few hundred dollars. Nothing that I hadn't lost a dozen times before. And after sixteen years of attachment parenting my two darling daughters, I was so very, very ripe for some grown-up fun. So ripe I was falling out of my tree.

"I'll be your dancer," said Kristin, raising her arms overhead and swirling her hips in a tantalizing sway. "I could play tambourine!" Perfect hippy instrument, it went right along with her wide-legged organic hemp yoga pants and her moldavite pendant from another galaxy. Our audience would be in for a trippy treat with Kristin onboard, her megawatt smile and winsome energy always at the ready.

With Deborah and Kristin cheering me on, suddenly, I had to follow through with my wild idea. There's nothing like speaking your dreams out loud to wrestle them into action. We all started taking lessons at Rhythm Fire, the local school of rock. I had driven past it for years, imagining impossibly hip people doing incredibly cool things inside. Crossing the hallowed threshold, I found Rhythm Fire to be a typical two-story house, except that in every room instead of couches and framed photos of granny, there was an instrument and a poster of Janis Joplin or Jimi Hendrix screaming their lungs out. Who needs couches?

Our friend Palu joined as guitarist and showed us what a band rehearsal looked like, because we literally did not have a clue where to start or what to do. How do you approach a song from scratch? Who goes first? What is the etiquette? Palu plugged mysterious cords into mysterious amps and produced most satisfying shrieks of feedback. And then we took a smoke break. The fact that we all shared one cigarette and felt slightly sick afterwards did nothing to dispel the glamorous aura enveloping us (or perhaps it was the smoke). Finally, we felt like real musicians.

In August, Palu left the band. It was all very amicable; we were going in different directions musically. We doubt very much whether it had anything to do with that field trip the band took to the local sex store, Lover's Package, to check out their scanty knickers (he didn't look *that* uncomfortable, crouched back there by the flavored lube display). He took his Ramones records and the Ramones wig I gave him and went back to his Batcave, where he hasn't been heard from since.

His desertion saddened the rest of the band for, oh, about ten minutes, until Deborah found the silver lining, as she tends to, pointing out that now we could be an ALL-GIRL BAND. Probably every lass's dream since she was nine years old, jumping on the bed to the Bangles. Yay! We're going down to Liverpool to do nothing, all the days of our lives!

Add Three Girls and Shake
by Kristin

Rain and I used to hang out together eight years ago in San Diego. Back then she wore multiple shades of gray, was married and shopped at the military PX. When her marriage dissolved, we were both in Washington, both with young families needing a place to live. We rented adorable cabins on the same land, holding each other and healing, our kids became as close as brothers and sisters. I would do anything for her. I have always been attracted to her stories, as she is an expert at noticing the fine details and putting them into writing. I felt her pain because she documented all of it - the nitty gritty and the grace.

As Rain found her mojo, she began sporting knee-high rock star boots in various colors and dyed her hair platinum. One day she asked me a question that was to change our lives. We were rocking out to the The Charlatans UK in her room and she was playing air drums. With a pretend drumstick in her hand, she sputtered between lyrics, "I am starting a rock band, I am not getting any younger. Are you in?" A week later she began drumming classes at a local hot spot for novice and professional performers, Rhythm Fire School of Music.

I had known this chick for more than a decade and this wasn't a military wife talking anymore. Rain was empowered and in the mood to rock. Me? Well, I am along for the ride because I have always seen myself on stage rousing a crowd and I know it is about to get craaaaazy.

Deborah is my co-singer and is learning how to play guitar. Prolific poet, Law of Attraction aficionado, mother of six with a voice that yearns to "Tell Me Something Good..." Deb is a minx. Magnetic attraction is what this woman naturally possesses and when the three of us hang out, it is akin to a spiritual awakening.

Just Say Yes
by Deborah

Rain and I met at a homeschooling cooperative in Olympia. There among the ultra-conservative moms, we were best friends from hello. Rain was artistic, funny, intelligent and read memoirs as voraciously as I did. While our kids took cooking and science classes, we traded stories, seeking out little nooks in the run-down building which housed the school program. We talked about music, movies, men and which math curriculum was best. More importantly, we were both trying on the cloak of positive thinking. It is hard to find kindred spirits in this department, especially among burnt-out moms who are with their children twenty-four/seven.

Six months after I met Rain, I adopted my youngest boys from Ethiopia (these two brought me to an even half dozen kiddos). In the meantime, my marriage ended and I fell in love with a newly divorced man. It was a trifecta of anxiety and my fleeting moments with Rain saved me - while I thrashed, she waved her magic wand, showering me with humor and affirmations that everything would be okay. I remember a critical moment when my new boys were misbehaving, my five-year-old was riding piggy back, squirming to get down while his brother ran away from me in the parking lot. I screamed, "What have I fucking done, my life is over, I can't do this!" Rain (using a beguiling British accent) replied, "Aw, ducky, don't worry about all that, sometimes it's enough just to make it until tea time."

The next time I saw Rain she offered me a madcap idea - she was forming a band. Was I in? My life was completely insane, it seemed crazy not to. In the past, I had taken guitar lessons but stopped every time I had a baby. I would master a few chords and then quit, using lack of hours and sleep as an excuse. At forty-two, I felt if I ever wanted to actualize this dream of mine, to sing while I played guitar, time (which I'd never had anyway) was no longer a reason. My Arbor acoustic, which I had moved from house to house, had been patiently waiting for two decades. Having someone to be accountable to, plus have fun with, was the missing ingredient all those years.

Rain soon introduced me to Kristin, the fairy sprite she had been telling me about, and I was instantly entranced by her bright sanguine spirit and generous heart. I started taking lessons again. It felt incredibly healthy to give myself a smidgen of the resources I gave my family. I'd poured countless hours and money into my own kids' musical hobbies and talents: at the time they played cello, guitar, drums and one was counting down the days until he turned ten so he could begin saxophone. I turned our formal living room into an official music room, bought a microphone and something to plug it into.

The band quickly became a necessary pressure valve. It, and the friendship we formed, was the one constant in a life that was evolving quicker than fruit flies in a petri dish. I had always coached others to follow their yearnings and suddenly I was flirting with mine, one chord, one note at a time.

How to Name Your Girl Band
by Deborah

A few months into our musical mystery trip, the girls and I were feeling mischievous and decided we needed a band retreat. The token male had abandoned us and we felt a bit unsteady, thinking "Wow, if the only real musician doesn't want to be with us, perhaps we should quit while we're ahead." But we didn't. We grabbed my RV, headed to Safeway to stock up on the four major food groups (red wine, chocolate, cheese and crackers) and ventured to Union, a small town forty-five minutes from Olympia. Kristin had heard there was a blues band playing at the grange. Now the word "grange" would stop most gals right there, but this was early on, and knowing what we know now (and that our first gig would be at the Black Lake Grange, there are no accidents...), we'd have gone anyway.

The parking lot was empty, but for a few pickups and some young bucks milling around out front. We can't swear we saw a confederate flag in one of the trucks, but it had that feel. We pulled our rig out front and reconnoitered. None of us were drawn to check out the music, so we opened the wine and had a huddle instead. We brought up the subject of our band name, Skanty Knickers, the tongue-in-cheek name Rain had originally come up with, was out and we were tossing around the name Pearl. We liked the symbolism, the simplicity of one word, that a pearl is the way a creature makes lemonade out of lemons, but the association with Seattle band Pearl Jam was haunting us and we just weren't *jazzed*. Minx was also in the running.

Another word that felt good in the mouth, but we didn't want a primarily sexual vibe with our name.

I remember the moment exactly when "Violet" was first mentioned. Rain said, "Well, my friend's daughter, Violet..." Immediately, my third eye lit up. I gasped, "VIOLET... Wow, what about that name?!"

As we pondered, I got a call from a friend who was in Seattle at Bumbershoot, where big name musicians were playing to thousands of people, Courtney Love being a headliner. We had brought along Courtney's book, *Dirty Blonde*, a scrapbook memoir. We wondered if we could make it up there in two hours, find a place to park the RV and catch a bit of this devilish diva. The wine had just kicked in though, so we decided to chill and experiment with my computer's photo booth, taking pictures of the three of us. We pondered the name for a few weeks after that seminal night. Violet stuck, obviously. Here are some guidelines that worked for us:

1. Be open to anything, be silly, watch for omens that you are on the right track. Courtney Love was ours, she seemed to be our patron saint that night. We thought her band name, Hole, was pretty darn clever and provocative. When we googled her, we found one of her most popular songs is named "Violet." Even though I don't resonate with the whole tune, I like the opening verse which talks about the sky being made of amethyst and all the stars, like little fish.
2. The name should mean something to you. Violet is a color we all love, we like that in the chakra system it is the highest

hue, corresponding to the crown of the head. We are all shrinking violets a bit, introverted writers who shyly bloom every now and again.

3. Talk to people about the name. See what their reactions are. Minx really excited the men, and sure we don't mind a bit of titillation, but didn't want that to be the primary association. Some folks thought we said "violent" as in "violence," which we were all right with, as we all feel a little violent sometimes, especially when we have been without music for a while.

4. Search the name on the internet. For Violet, there is a band called Violette but they haven't done much in the last few years and are in Australia. See if you can get something close to your name for a domain name and email as well.

5. Think about branding. Is there a consistent image that goes with the name? Think the Rolling Stones with their pop-art open mouth. In our case it is the color and the flower.

6. Consider your audience. Our original name, Skanty Knickers, was sassy and fun, especially as we all like to talk in English accents, but our kids were embarrassed by it. One of our favorite local bands is called Missionary Position, a bold name on their part, but not exactly PG-rated. We wanted a name we could use anywhere, with anyone.

Fun Violet Fluff:

Psychics who claim to be able to observe the aura with their third eye report that those who are practicing occultists often have a violet aura.

It is said that people with violet auras are forward-looking visionaries who may have occupations such as performance artist, photographer, venture capitalist, astronaut, futurist, or quantum physicist.

In Chinese painting, the color violet represents the harmony of the universe because it is a combination of blue and red (yin and yang respectively).

True violets have been known for centuries, with the ancient Greeks cultivating them about 500 BC. Both the Greeks and the Romans used violets for all sorts of things, such as for herbal remedies, wine (Vinum Violatum), to sweeten food and for festivals.

The ancient Greeks considered the flower violet a symbol of fertility and love and used them in love potions. Their symbolism is modesty, virtue, affection, watchfulness, faithfulness, love and my favorite of all, "let's take a chance on happiness."

Photo Shoot
by Kristin

One salty, frothy, sultry Saturday night, we vixen goddesses decided to go out in the Winnebago-esque motor home that Deborah keeps in her driveway for soul adventures. Our goal that night was to check out local talent; however, we ended up having our first photo shoot and coming up with the name Violet. The back room in "Winnie" is where it all began for us.

Rain was picture ready, rocking her hairdo as only she can. Deborah and I recently voted Rain "most photogenic" of the three of us. I secretly look forward to band practice every week because I want to see what Rain has done with her golden mane. Is it teased or in long curly ringlets? Rain reminds me of Kristen Stewart, in the biopic, *The Runaways*. Stewart is hot and it is her hair. Am I the only one who imagines running my fingers through her silky shag? I think not.

Up until this point in the evening, Deborah was wearing her summer play clothes: cut-offs, a faded t-shirt and gold sandals. Then she opened a portal in "Winnie" to the tiniest closet imaginable, and nonchalantly plucked a zebra-striped, floor-length, sleeveless dress off a violet hanger. I reaffirmed my own choice of outfit, a heart-stopping mauve mini, and sank back into the bed. It was on!

When no one was looking, Deborah had schooled herself in using her laptop to expertly stage a photo shoot. "Kristin, cross your arms in front of you, Rain, nice arch of your brow!" I am constantly cutting out pictures in music magazines. Plastered on my walls and in my mind are images of the Yeah, Yeah, Yeahs, the Gossip, India.Arie and old photos of Joan Jett and the Blackhearts. Girl bands are especially yum. I was channeling Regina Spektor. My "dream board" was coming alive. We each had a sense of how we wanted future shoots to go. We were merely playing at this point, but when the time comes to create postcards and Violet concert posters, we will be ready!

There we were creating our dream in the Skokomish Grange parking lot, where we thought we'd gone to listen to music but were greeted in the driveway by kids flattening beer cans on their heads.

Princess of Percussion
by Rain

Deborah loosened her purse strings, as her generous soul so often does, and gave me my very first drum lesson at the age of forty-eight. I was delighted to hear my teacher would be a woman. When you are shut in a room with someone and you are feeling particularly vulnerable (think hairdresser, gynecologist, or music teacher), it's nice to have something in common with them, like a vagina. *Princess of Percussion*, Darlene's business card reads. When you call her number, a rat-a-tat drum sounds in the background as she chortles, "I'm on a roll - leave a message!" I've learned a lot from her in just a few lessons. "Never sit at a drum set without a beat in your head," she advises. "And get used to using a metronome!"

I started out practicing on my bed pillows until Darlene found me a decent drum kit on craigslist. Heaven for only $275, and she let me pay her back in installments. She must get a kick out of another woman loving the skins as much as she does. Can anyone be a drummer? I'm not sure. I picked the drums as my instrument on a whim, but I have always played air drums along with the car stereo, much to the consternation of my passengers. At my first lesson, I was hugely relieved when Darlene observed, "You keep excellent time. You'll make a fine drummer."

I highly recommend taking a few lessons, because as with any instrument, it's easy to acquire bad habits that can be murder to break later on. Darlene taught me how to hold my drumsticks, for example, never letting my thumbs wander past my index fingers. She showed me how to lift my whole leg to pound the bass pedal, instead of just my foot. She also schooled me on tuning the drums with a special key, and how to break down a kit for transport.

The holy grail for a new drummer is Limb Separation, a mystical process whereby each limb can play a different rhythm. At first it seems laughably impossible. But slowly, new neural pathways are hacked through the jungle of under-used brain cells, and you reach an oasis of syncopation. Aaaaaahhh. Now the fun can begin. In fact, I think that is precisely why drumming makes me happy - it engages both sides of my brain simultaneously. And loudly.

I love it best when Darlene helps me learn a new song. She leaps up and sails around the room, her long hair flapping behind her. "Thunk thunk thunk. Hear the bass?" She crosses her fingers. "You're like that. That's your buddy. Follow him." She listens closely to the first verse, then grabs her sticks and starts approximating the basic beat, throwing in fills and rolls. I gamely try to follow her on my side-by-side drum kit. "Write it down," I beg, knowing when I get home, my tenuous grasp will have evaporated like fairy dust. The half-hour lesson whizzes by in what seems like minutes. Darlene, Princess of Percussion, Lady A-Leaping, jumps up to start the track over one last time, and pauses by the controls. "Should I turn it up?" she says.

Like she had to ask.

THE MISSIONARY POSITION AND I
BY RAIN

One Saturday night, I found myself with four dollars to my name and a deep craving for release. All two of my friends were otherwise engaged and unavailable for havoc-wreaking. I steeled my nerve and determined, I AM GOING TO WALK INTO A BAR ALL BY MYSELF, STONE-COLD SOBER. Mind you, for shy me, this pronouncement could have been accompanied by footage of Armstrong on the moon. That's how far-out the idea was. But there was a carrot dangling in front of my space helmet, and that carrot was a band from Seattle called The Missionary Position, who were set to play at the Fourth Avenue Tavern ("Fourth Ave Tav" to initiates) that very night. Cover charge: four dollars. Kismet.

I knew nothing of the band save the name, which had caught my eye on flyers. The Missionary Position. C'mon. Do you think the girl who wanted to name her band Skanty Knickers was going to pass this up? Not bloody likely. What a double bill that would have made... but I digress.

I threw on what I like to think of as my "Courtney Love" dress: long, black, with taffeta trim and just a hint of kinderwhore. I strapped on my Victorian ankle boots, teased out my Marilyn hair, slapped on some eyeliner and, with a double swipe of deodorant, headed out the door. Ten minutes later, I pulled up right in front of the bar. I love Olympia - everything happens on two streets, Fourth and Fifth, and there's always front-row parking.

I took a deep breath, wobbled in, paid the cover and showed my ID. At my age, I weep with joy that they're still asking. I made a beeline past the gauntlet of men on bar stools. No eye contact.   I marched similarly past those even scarier men, the ones playing pool. This was very far from the new wave clubbing I had done about a hundred years ago, BC (Before Children). Where was George Michael when I needed him? Probably across the street at the gay disco, Jake's. I was on my own.

I entered a small, murky back room, where there were exactly eight people. I eyed them carefully. Four of them must be in the band I deduced, judging by their all-black clothing and air of purpose. I perched at one of those high bistro tables where you're neither standing nor sitting, but sort of *leaning*, and tried to look like I hung out at bars regular-like, and that my heart wasn't beating like a two-fisted self-pleasurer.

Wait a minute. The band is in the audience? Not secreted away in some green room, snorting coke off groupies' implants? My imaginary rock scene splintered around me and I peered into the much more fascinating world of the journeyman musician.

The band took to the tiny stage and rewarded this courageous space adventurer with three-plus hours of primo rock 'n' roll. The keyboardist and drummer, both in stocking feet and beatific expressions, were clearly channeling from a different dimension. The saxophonist held down his corner with a thick stream of soul. And the frontman? He commanded the space with charisma to burn, growling out darkly romantic lyrics while kicking his mike stand down and back up and even playing lead guitar, excellently, with it. The music was a genre-bending cross between Motown and Nine Inch Nails. I was riveted to the spot, willing the vibe to build and build, which it did. I could not believe the band was giving their all, which was a considerable amount, to a handful of rather reserved people. Surely someone was going to break down and toss their panties in appreciation at any second. But... no. At least, I don't think I did.

The lead singer said little besides "thank you" between songs, so his deadpan trash-talk after each set came as a bonus. "It's late, so if you couldn't afford a babysitter and your baby's asleep in the car, now might be a good time to change him. I'd like to direct you to our merch table, where we are selling t-shirts suitable for use."

During the first break, I zipped up my spacesuit and gingerly approached the drummer by the merch (merchandise, I learned) table. He looked uber-hip in his skinny jeans and hair gel. Do rock musicians from the big city bark, bite, or merely sneer? I quickly learned, none of the above.

"I like your drumming," I began.
"Thank you, and thank you for saying so." He smiled and gave me his full attention.
"You look like you're having the time of your life up there," I continued.

I heard myself saying, "I play drums, too" and we were off. Musician to musician, not rock star to sycophant. Shoulder to shoulder, drumstick to drumstick. Except I can't do that twirly thing with mine yet. Another set, another break, and at one a.m., they were still pumping, but I had to leave. I had a heinous seven a.m. wake up call awaiting me. On my way out, I passed the lead singer, who was taking a breather, and offered my hand to thank him.

He prolonged the clasp. Tattoos rippled on sinuous skin and glossy black hair curled where it was soaked with sweat, my keen journalistic eye noted. He flashed his full charm at me. Which was a considerable amount.

"I can't convince you to stay? The next set is a quiet one, I promise..."

To infinity and beyond, Neil!

Why Everyone Should Have a Stage Name
by Deborah

When the band was tossing around titles as readily as we tossed back cosmopolitans, we decided to take on musical monikers. Speaking of cosmos, they fit our mood at the time, a brief rebellion that usually meant we were tired and cranky the next day, which we soon realized doesn't fly when one has a family to take care of in the morning. It is one thing to be a rock star and sleep in a hotel room or tour bus until noon, one thing to have the metabolism of a twenty-year-old. In reality, our imbibing was on par with most women's book clubs, in terms of alcohol consumed (and expletives exchanged), but we did make it through with playful alter-ego names.

They are cheeky, as was Rain's original band name of Skanty Knickers, which no doubt was the result of her watching too much British comedy. But Kristin and I were on board. Kristin chose KaryzMa! (yes, with an exclamation point and capital "M"). Rain chose Swallow, a naughty or nice name, "Like the bird, of course. Swallows come out to play at twilight, like I do," she demurely admonishes anyone with raised eyebrows.

I adopted a similarly saucy name, Goldilicks, a bastardization of Goldilocks, for my crazy peroxide-induced gold curls and licks being guitar licks, naturally. The slight sexual reference did not escape us, nor any man I was introduced to as such. Fun for about a week. Then I fell head over heels in love, cleaned up my post-divorce act and shortened my nomenclature to Goldi.

Cher. Bono. Sting. Madonna. Adelle. Macklemore. Lorde.

They stick for a reason. The cool thing is any time my girls call me Goldi, which they often do, I giggle, reminding myself that even if I have not achieved my potential, somewhere in there is a bliss bombshell waiting to emerge.

BAND RESEARCH
BY RAIN

Deborah and I have begun to do Band Research. BR we call it for short. We tried taking Kristin along, but by eleven p.m. her eyelids were drooping and she listed gently on her bar stool. She has been temporarily reassigned to Print Media Band Research. Translation: she finds radical bands in *Bust* and *Spin* magazines. During daylight hours.

We like to venture out into the dark of night to see what the moon goddess has to offer. While this may appear to the, ahem, naked eye as mere licentious carousing, it is in fact a carefully executed plan to carouse licentiously while discovering how other bands line up *gigs*, sell *merch*, compose *set lists*, and other arcane, yet vital band matters.

We don't really do this as often as we should. Boyfriends, ex-husbands, jobs, errands, flossing, and what are those again? Oh, yes - children - tend to eat up a lot of time. But every month or so, Deborah hurtles her golden chariot (cleverly disguised as a Dodge minivan) down my driveway and ferries me to the Other Side. *Come to the dark side - we have cookies* as the bumper sticker says, or in Deborah's case, vodka, ice and organic lemonade in a giant tupperware vat. Deborah, I suspect, is the love child of Martha Stewart and Dionysus.

We make a pit stop at the Shell station for Black and Milds ("They don't make your fingers stink," counsels Deborah), Turkish Gold Camels for stinky-fingered Rain, and Cheetos and Reese's Cups for those afterglow munchies.

The other night was a high-water mark in our BR so far. First, we went to the Fourth Ave Tav to scope out The Missionary Position. I'd been blown away by them before and wanted to share the joy with Deborah. We were at the bar when I noticed the tall, lean, muscular man with a world of hurt in his eyes, standing behind us, was none other than Jeff Angell, the lead singer.

"You're Jeff Angell," I suavely blurted out. And he agreed, as how could he not.

"We're buying your drink, of course," said Deborah (smooth!). A Red Bull. Turns out he is clean and sober. He was getting a pitcher of water for the band. We introduced ourselves ("We're in a girl band called Violet"), and somehow started talking about song-writing and inspiration for lyrics.

"I'm always at it, looking for lines," he remarked observantly. "Writers are vampires," I observed remarkably.

The band took the stage for a blistering two-and-a-half-hour set (note to self: clean and sober musicians don't need smoke or pee breaks, apparently). Deborah fetched the band another jug of well-earned water while I fielded dramatic texts from my eleven-year-old tweenager.

Tween: MAMA I NEED U I FELL DOWN DANCING MY HIP HURTS WHERE R U???
Me: Take an ibuprofen honey and put an icepack on it. I am doing Band Research.

We learned that after the show, if you lurk around the merch table, you may actually get invited to an after-party, like we did. But since the band wasn't going, we decided not to, either. Deborah, however, got the lead singer's phone number. Here's how she did it: "I sing lead vocals, too. Can you teach me how to do what you do?" Bat bat bat of the eyelashes. Smooth. Nah, she's sincere, too.

After the show, Deborah and I wandered out onto the sidewalk to await instructions from Goddess Flow (not to be confused with Goddess Flo, who can usually be found, if needed, at a diner on Route 66). Sure enough, two guys strolled by and remarked on the sublime scent of our Black and Milds (note to self: musicians are a generous breed, always glad to share your last cigarette with you). They were members of a Seattle band called Reckless Nomad, who had just played their first Oly gig, at The Pig (which might actually have another name, but it's most recognizable by its neon sign of - you guessed it - a pink pig).

"It was awesome!" crowed the singer/guitarist, Adam. "We just got paid $195 cash, they fed us, free drinks, everything! This is way better than Seattle, where you practically have to pay them to let you play." The bass player, Kyle, was even more jubilant. It was his first gig with the band since picking up the bass only a month before. He had also booked the gig, after seeing a craigslist ad exactly one day ago. To the fleet go the spoils. Noting to ourselves and justifying even more BR - check craigslist and insist on free drinks.

We bought their CD (heavy Hendrix vibe) out of the back of their car, after tromping around a little in the freezing cold, searching for where they had parked it ("I'm pretty sure it was on this street somewhere...").

Awash with sensory input, Deborah and I wound up at another Olympia two a.m. tradition, the Gyro Stand, ready for a little grounding, or at least ground lamb. The two gyro guys were just packing up, but agreed to make us one last sandwich. We all sang "I Want To Hold Your Hand" and they invited us to have our first show at their stand. Busking in Olytown! As we were leaving, Trevor, whose gray eyes could level a skyscraper, gave me a hug goodnight. He lifted me clear off the ground and cracked my spine all the way down.

It felt great. All of it.

Groupies, Not Gropies
by Deborah

I had my first experience as a groupie last Saturday night. Rain and I were among a small throng of devotees watching Missionary Position (MP for brevity's sake), crank out yet another night of amazing music and heart. Wait, I think we were the only devotees. MP does have a small following in Olympia, but Rain and I are definitely the most enthusiastic fans.

Rain had gone on and on about MP when she first saw them perform, so it didn't take much to get me to the next show, especially when she told me about Jeff Angell, the front man, writing love letters to his pubescent daughter in red ink, to give to her on her first menses (Rain had heard this in an interview). MP was as good as she said. My favorite tunes were an original heart-crushing ballad called "All My Mistakes" and the best cover of Prince's "Erotic City" I have ever heard. Speaking of erotic, I must admit it didn't even take the second beer for me to be curious if the way Jeff handled his guitar translated into how he might handle other instruments (where the gropie part comes in). We chatted between sets and he proved every bit as charming, as talented on stage.

Hooking up with the front man was not my intention, but the possibility didn't seem so far off, especially when during a keyboard solo, Jeff came off the stage and twirled me around the dance floor. However, what Rain and I really wanted was to connect as fellow musicians with Jeff and his crew.

The second time we saw them in Olympia, we headed over to the merch table and bought t-shirts, putting them on over our tops. A bit gropie and a bit groupie. I had already bought the CD at the last show, and rationalized the t-shirts might cover MP's gas at least halfway back to Seattle. Here are a few things we have learned in our limited experience:

1. Don't hang out after the show trying to hook up - tacky. That's what gropies do. Groupies have their own lives and bands enhance it, not ARE it. Even though both nights Rain and I were up for a little more mischief, we let them have their space.

2. It's okay to throw out a bone and see if there is a nibble. I asked Jeff if he gave voice lessons. He seemed interested in sharing his insights and on his own, offered me the MP business card with his cell number on the back. I never called, as life got busy, but the next time I saw MP, Jeff remembered me.

3. It's all right to be a groupie, as in go to lots of shows - if you are really interested in supporting the band, they love it. Another time, my S.O. and I (yes, I brought my Significant Other which immediately killed any chance I had with Jeff) joined Rain to see MP at a jazzy lounge in the Sorrento Hotel in Seattle. As the night wore on, the stuffy older crowd finished their martinis and left and the hipsters, wearing skinny jeans and lots of black eyeliner, appeared. Jeff noticed us and signaled from the stage as he sang, then came over and schmoozed for a while between sets, genuinely glad to see us all. It felt lovely - respect and admiration clinking all around.

Brother Skyler
by Deborah

We have been off to a rough start in the starting a band business. Rain broke her toe and Kristin was on a road trip, I cut my left pointer finger badly, curtailing my beginning guitar attempts and the winter holidays in general had us busted busy. We kept talking about music though, and were ready to build on what we had started back in the spring.

We felt we needed to kick it up a notch and hired Skyler, a musical genius who puts together bands at Rhythm Fire. He himself plays several instruments and sings, one-stop shopping for us, none of this would be happening without him. At first, we were shy violets, still barely able to hold our instruments correctly, but Skyler admired our courage for even trying. We were delighted that he let us leap right in with a song rather than torturing us for months with scales. During our very first lesson, Skyler focused on us finding and feeling *the groove.*

Today we brought him two songs we wanted to work on, "Loving Cup" by the Rolling Stones and "You Give Me Something" by James Morrison. He listened to both of them and gave his thumbs up, "You can definitely cover them and find your own interpretation." Code: "You can't do it as well as them, as they are seasoned musicians, but let's give it a go!" Earlier he had gently steered us away from Chaka Khan's challenging "Tell Me Something Good." First rock, then soul.

In a few weeks, Rhythm Fire is having their quarterly showcase. The kids' bands will be performing, and we decided to have something prepared, otherwise we could stay in limbo land forever. There is only so much Band Research and looking for fab rock star clothing a gal can do. We have been working on "Can't Let Go" by Lucinda Williams and we asked Skyler about using the keyboard as bass after we saw Missionary Position do just that. He picked out the notes as I snapped off a few photographs of the classic band posters in his studio.

In no time, Skyler had Kristin on keyboard, I was given a strum pattern for my guitar and Rain had a steady beat on the drum. For a prelude to the actual song, we tried an exercise I am sure he has his ten-year-old students do, following a simple chord progression, G-C-G-C-D-G over and over. It was as basic as it gets, but it was music; for the first time, we all felt it! I am sure the fourth graders he works with don't get half as excited as we did.

The First Time Around Wasn't So Pretty
by Kristin

I quit the flute in fifth grade after two months of lessons. If I close my eyes, I can go back to being eleven years old when my teacher would tell all the band kids to go to the music room. My stomach gurgled and groaned all morning before her announcement. The whole hour of class, I watched the clock tick, as I knew I did not want to play the flute pretty much after the third or fourth lesson. The misery was compounded when we started learning how to read music. I was too embarrassed to ask my teacher questions because the other kids seemed to understand lightning quick. With every minute that passed, my heart beating loudly, my palms sweaty, I felt more and more invisible. I dreaded practicing at home and instead would sit on my mom's bed and stare at myself in her bedroom mirror. It was my first memory of negative self-talk, a bitter seed I unconsciously planted.

Now twenty-five years later, I am attempting to play an instrument again. I've decided to try the keyboard. I have known that an instrument would build my self-confidence, as you use the left and right parts of your brain and for me, syncing them has always been a huge challenge. If you were to ask me today how I feel about learning to play, I would tell you it is hard. I would tell you that many times I intend to buckle down and practice and then do not. It has been a lesson about getting out of my comfort zone.

My husband and I went to the Guitar Center a couple of weeks ago and I found a used, yet sleek Yamaha keyboard. It shines, it beckons to me. I bribe myself by practicing in my jammies, nude or pretending I am a rock star and dressing the part. My hubby is a natural and loves to give me pointers, trying to help find the best learning styles for me. My six-year-old son, Coletrane, is a coach and an inspiration as well. He pokes me, he prods me and I will be damned if I am going to let him see me repeat history.

I almost had a breakdown at band practice last time, working on Lucinda William's song "Can't Let Go." I could not keep up with Rain and Deborah and felt my insecure eleven-year-old dig her toes into the floor. My heart flew through my chest and tears welled up. But then I took a deep breath, and decided now was the time to slay that old self-loathing inner dragon. I did what I didn't do when I was eleven, I asked for help. Skyler went through the song chord by chord, while I watched his finger placement, not sure I could ever master it.

As we left the lesson, I confessed to the girls, "I was scared because I couldn't get it." I went home and did not practice, laid in my bed staring at the keyboard, not able to touch it.

And God Created Rock 'n' Roll
by Rain

All of my life, I have studied rock 'n' roll like meteorologists study tornados. *Tiger Beat* magazine was my teenage bible. David Cassidy! His shaggy haircut, bell-bottom jeans and lazy smile said *Danger, Danger, Warning* to me, and the call of freedom in a Partridge Family tour bus was irresistible. Musicians just seemed to have more FUN than the rest of us. Put it this way - there were no magazines devoted to account- ants and their celebration of the good life.

I am old enough now to see the bigger picture, how music responds to the world, and offers what it needs. Then the pendulum swings again, and what was in is suddenly out, or vice versa. This year's fashion of neon colors and positive boy bands like One Direction comes after a period of moody *Twilight* darkness, just as when I was twenty and Wham! bopped onto the world stage like Mexican jumping beans, relieving us of the darkness that punk had devolved into. With that in mind, here's my version of:

The History of Rock 'n' Roll

And on the seventh day God rested. He had created the word, the stars and the planets, the birds and beasties and the people. And all of that was very tiring. So he had Himself a proper lie-up.

And while He was relaxing, He had this niggling feeling that He had left something out. Something quite essential to the rhythm of the whole scheme. Something ephemeral, yet vital. Something... fun.

So on the eighth or maybe ninth day, probably on a Saturday night after payday, God created Muddy Waters and Robert Johnson and Buddy Holly in the backwaters of the Mississippi Delta (okay, okay, Buddy Holly was really from Lubbock, Texas).

And highly-photogenic teenage boys on the island kingdom of Great Britain in the 1950's heard this and saw that it was good. They wore their 45 rpm record needles down to nubs as they tried to reproduce chord progressions, harmonica moans, and that sound cats make when you step on their tails.

These Johns and Pauls and Micks and Keiths crossed the Great Pond known as the Atlantic and brought the gospel of rock 'n' roll to the starving masses. And there was much weeping and gnashing of teeth and, especially, rending of garments. Inevitably, hotel rooms got trashed. Shoes got taller and shirts got smaller. And this henceforth became known as *the Sixties*.

And tabs of acid magically multiplied among the multitudes and there was much growing of hair: head hair, and facial hair, and, yea, even unto armpit hair (and that was just the women). There was navel-gazing and trippy trips to India and subsequent dysentery. The troubadours began to play long, bloated, technically flawless guitar solos, and suddenly it was *the Seventies*, and rock 'n' roll had ascended to a rarefied realm of Tudor mansions, Lear jets, and drowning in pools of other people's vomit.

So then, 'round about 1975, God created the Sex Pistols. He gave them safety pins and hair dye and said unto them, "Give the music back to the people." And it is famously writ that only forty of the multitude, quite a small number, really, were present at the Sex Pistols' June 4, 1976 gig, but that every one of them immediately went out, stole a guitar and formed a band. Among the flock were future members of Joy Division, The Fall, The Smiths, Buzzcocks... and Jon the Postman.

And thus in the crucible of Northern England a new aesthetic was born. A do-it-yourself sensibility that spread throughout the western world by way of a Sunday night MTV show, *120 Minutes*, which was on so late only insomniacs and the unemployed could ever watch it. And this was called *alternative* music. And it was good.

This percolated nicely underground for the next ten years or so while various *hair* and *metal* bands filled the arenas with... well, hair and metal, mostly. Until, in 1991, God verily said, "Let Nirvana's *Nevermind* rise to the number one spot on the Billboard album charts." And hipsters listened in wonder that fated morning and they were smote with awe. Some seismic, tectonic shift had taken place. What could it mean? Could it be, as R.E.M predicted, "The end of the world as we know it"? Anyway, I felt fine.

There is much debate in religious circles whether, at this point, God in fact said, "Let there be Milli Vanilli," or if it was just a really loud belch.

By now the womenfolk had gotten royally fed up with misogynist lyrics and groping mosh pits and decided to adopt the punk ethic and become Riot Grrrls. And verily they proved they could manage three chords and dripping irony just as well as their brethren.

Now we arrive at the present day of pyrotechnic mega-concerts and inflated talent shows. I, for one, think it's high time God said something along the lines of "Let there be no more of lip-syncing, airbrushing or publicists, and once again, give the music back to the people!"

Amen (belch).

Let It Bleed
by Deborah

I am listening to the Rolling Stones
at the Dollar Store,
not your usual muzak playing over the radio,
here is Mick Jagger himself
in the uncensored version of the song "Let It Bleed,"
singing about dreaming on and
creaming on
and bleeding on

and what amazes me is no one is paying attention,
not to the music or me as I sway
with my cart in the gift wrap section,
grooving past a whole row
of cheap cardboard shirt boxes
and shiny hologram gold and cobalt gift bags,
no one is noticing as they place
their generic gum in their baskets,
as they turn over the thinnest glass snow globes.

I pet a lady as I move past her,
can't help myself, I let my hand linger
and she moves in,
as if she hasn't been touched in a decade,
our exchange is an epiphany, it's the Second Coming,
it's better than real Crest toothpaste
for a buck in the next aisle over.

I realize what Mick is preaching is all I've ever been,
it's what I've been afraid to say
that I am a pillow, a condom, a bandage
begging the world, *Use Me.*

I am drunk with it, while checking out,
become an amoeba merging
with the helium balloons
that will deflate in an hour,
with the hacking housewife behind me.
I offer myself to the reeking homeless man
whose nose is dripping.
I flirt with him and pay the 1.09 he doesn't have
as his food stamps don't cover buying disposable razors,

and everyone in the dollar store line is grossed out
and he's looking at me like I am the Madonna,
like my halo is glitter sparkly,
but I brush it off, lie
and tell him I've been helped out in line before.
He chortles after me as I run to my car in the rain,
"Hey! You got some fries with that shake?"
I laugh and nod wildly and think of Mick,
still strutting on stage in his sixties,
think to myself,

Do I ever.

What Goes Around
by Kristin

One of my first encounters with my husband Michael was around music, although we haven't shared much of it in our relationship. That is, until recently, with the arrival of Violet. I met Michael when he was a vegan chef in San Diego. He was also a guitar player, and he invited me to watch him perform to raw foodie enthusiasts in the cafe section of a new co-op. Michael forgot the cord to his electric guitar and was forced to strum along unplugged, complete with his hairnet and a sideways smile. Hilarious.

Prior to that evening, I had tried to pawn him off on various friends that I thought he would be good with. My childhood buddy Vicki was my most recent victim. Halfway through the set she looked at me with her tiger-like eyes and said, "Oh, darling, stop trying to give that boy away to your girlfriends... it is so obvious that he is for you!" She encouraged me to buy him a drink after his show and the rest is history.

The first time I sang in front of Michael was on our way home from a Christmas party. I was slightly buzzed and Bob Marley came on the radio. Many regard Bob as a God of sorts - Michael and I are no exception. I began making up words to his song, which is what I do when I don't know them. Michael was driving and when he heard me mumble nonsense, he pulled over to the side of the road, stood in front of the headlights and jumped up and down in frustration. I got out and asked him what was going on. He had only been a soft-spoken Renaissance man thus far, but not tonight. "What are you doing, Kristin?! You cannot just make up words to Bob's song, it isn't right. It is maddening!" I was dumbstruck.

It took me seven years, until I joined Violet, to sing out loud in front of him again. After an open mic at the restaurant he works at, I drove us home, singing along to the girl group, The Dixie Chicks. He touched my hand and said, "Darlin,' your voice is lovely." I never in a million years thought I would hear that coming from the man who practically ran us off the road when I sang his favorite song in a way that he did not approve of. His affirmation was heartfelt.

Soon thereafter, I began vocal lessons with Deborah at our music school, which further increased my confidence. I was able to pass along this gift of validation to my father. His wives (all three of them!) were never keen about him serenading, so the shower became his haven. At fifty-six, he is just beginning to sing in front of others. I love it when things come full circle, and with my hubby, the music has, as well. I am now even encouraging him to perform again, because despite his wooing me years ago, he claims to hate his singing voice. Crazy talk.

Keith Richards Meets Joy Division
by Rain

I have four younger brothers, all variations on a theme of sardonic, tolerant bachelors. At Christmas time, one or two of them generally comes through with a tasty present, and this year was a double-dipped literary delight. James offered the definitive, collector's edition of *Joy Division* from photographer Kevin Cummins, and a day later, *Life* by Keith Richards arrived along with my brother Gordon, in person.

I thumbed through the pictures first. *Joy Division* is crammed with 8x10 photos, all black and white, peeking into the days and moods of the fledgling Manchester band, circa 1977-1979. Stark rehearsal rooms are festooned with cigarette butts, cables and sweat. Are those leather pants on the usually elegant lead singer Ian Curtis? Surely not. Guess he rethought those early on. He is alternately intense and weary in every shot. Can we wonder, from the writer of "Love Will Tear Us Apart"? Such an ironic, poignant title.

Ian famously suffered from depression, no doubt complicated by the heavy medications prescribed for his recently-diagnosed epilepsy. The courage he exhibited, getting up on stage and never knowing if tonight would result in a grand mal seizure in public, is stunning.

In other shots, the band wanders through a snowy urban landscape. Cold. And that's how I remember feeling, for much of my early twenties. Cold, as I struggled to find my way and bands like Joy Division held my hand, hour by grim hour. In a trenchant foreword, Jay McInerney (*Bright Lights, Big City*) talks about the sadness we often feel as we leave our teenage years and become aware of the iniquities of the world at large. The sadness that caused Ian to take his own life at age twenty-three.

Keith Richards, on the other hand, defied the rock 'n' roll odds and is kicking up his heels (instead of the bucket) all these years later. On the jacket sleeve, he avows that he hasn't forgotten any of it. Hah! What kind of company is "Keef"? He's a gas, gas, gas. He's got the silver. He's a street-fighting man, a soul survivor. He's happy. Yes, he does appear somewhat torn and frayed around the edges. For many years, he slept, on average, twice a week. It's this manic energy that we have to thank for his super-human output as guitarist/songwriter/singer with the Rolling Stones. Album after album of bedrock music, deliciously dirty proto-grunge.

Keith hilariously relates a story where the band was meeting in the studio for writing/recording sessions. They started out convening at eight p.m., which quickly devolved to ten p.m., one a.m., four a.m. and so forth. One day he was being driven to the studio when he chanced to clock the time - eight a.m. He told the driver to turn around, that he couldn't possibly go to work that early.

This anarchic spirit informs every page of the book, and can perhaps be traced back to school days when, after winning a prestigious choir cup for his school, his voice broke and he was forced to repeat a year because he had missed so much school due to singing competitions. Thus, a rebel was born.

Keith's photos reveal a glamorous, high-flying, Technicolor life. Hounded by police and press, perhaps the most famous heroin addict this world has ever known, and, finally, immortalized for the Disney crowd by Johnny Depp's portrayal of the tipsy, canny Jack Sparrow in the *Pirates of the Caribbean* movies. What if Johnny Depp had chosen to play Jack Sparrow as Ian Curtis, instead? The movies would have had to be in black and white - no turquoise spangles on idyllic waters for Ian. Certainly no giggles, dreadlocks or treasure.

Or perhaps, treasure of a different sort. Buried very deep, twenty or thirty years ago, things you loved with all your heart and laid aside for a moment that turned into years. For me, it's a love of music, coaxed along by Ian, Keith, my brothers and others, that slaps a silly smile on my face and spills over onto grocery clerks and even dentists.

Follow the Bouncing Ball
by Deborah

Recently, Skyler, our music teacher/sage was up on the white board, tapping out some chord progressions for the song we were going to perform. He used a pointer while Kristin and I did our best to keep up with the steady metronome beat of Rain's drumming. We talked about how it was like karaoke - you sing the words as the little ball goes along, he quickly extrapolated this idea to life in general.

I have been trying to figuratively follow the bouncing ball for a few years now, ever since I went away to a retreat called The School. The School is a nine day immersion in letting go and letting God hosted by Byron Katie, a spiritual teacher, who wrote a book called *Loving What Is*. The premise of the book, like most spiritual tomes, is to be in the present moment, for it is all we have. Katie talked about a concept she called "following the simple directions," in which you follow your inner voice, asking yourself what feels right. As life choices present themselves, you simply feel, *yes or no*? That's it. No drama, not much planning, just following where your heart takes you.

I had a sweet example of this at The School, after I had just purchased a coral-colored pashmina scarf from the gift shop that I was really excited about. A staff member sat next to me and complimented me on it and I literally heard the simple directions, *give her the scarf*. I took the cloth I had been wearing around my neck for no more than an hour and handed it to her. She immediately burst into tears and hugged me. She didn't tell me anything about her experience, although at the break, I saw her talking earnestly to another staffer, stroking the soft fabric, her eyes still glistening. I didn't need to know her story or why that exchange was meaningful, the instant feedback was plenty.

"Do you want to be in a band, Deborah?" I was asked by Rain some time ago. Yes or no? *Yes*. And here we are...

Skyler paused before his teaching and said, "I can't talk about this with everyone I instruct, you guys get it on all levels, don't you?" We encouraged him earnestly. Kristin whipped out her journal and poised to take notes. Skyler continued, "Music, and I mean all of it, is a metaphor for life. It is a complete mirror, containing all lessons."

The girls and I have been putting this philosophy to the test, not stressing as our little Violet flower alternately blossoms and wilts. Even if we haven't been diligently practicing, we have been committed to at least our Band Research, following the crumbs, which has led us to many an inspiring time.

Here below, is the gospel, according to Skyler (and Buddha and the Tao and such modern mystics as Byron Katie and Eckhardt Tolle, author of *The Power of Now*):

1. It is all about the groove - there is no destination, you don't make music to have a final product and be done, it is about the experience of creating and being in present time.

2. Wax on, wax off - anyone who has seen *Karate Kid* remembers when the sensei had his student wax his car over and over, the same movements he would use for karate blocks and strikes. It is all about muscle memory. You must put in the time to train your body to change chords quickly, drum evenly, play those keys smoothly.

3. Follow the bouncing ball - don't get too far ahead of yourself, be in the moment, let life unfold. If we'd known how much work it was going to take to learn our instruments, we may have never kept going. But we are learning one chord, one song at a time. None of us might have had children, or gotten degrees, or published books if we had known the effort involved.

4. The less energy you can use, the more powerful you can be - in the beginning it takes a lot of concentration and muscle to change chords or to sing loudly, but as diaphragms and biceps develop, you become more efficient. Instead of lurching from one transition to another, you learn how to conserve energy, thus freeing your attention to experience deeply the sound you are making. This is true of all life. The other day, I whispered at my kids instead of yelling. I got their attention and didn't have the toxic hangover I usually do when I let loose on them.

5. There are no mistakes - play them loud and proud and learn from them, listen to how the wrong chord sounds. There is no perfection, only feel the "offness," own it, learn and move on.

6. Listen to yourself and others at the same time - any time you play with someone else, you have to be able to hear them and yourself simultaneously. Any good counseling

technique such as Non-Violent Communication teaches us to listen to the other person while also being present to our own experience. This is perhaps the most important of all of Skyler's, and life's lessons.

A FOREST DARK - THE SECOND ACT
BY RAIN

It is consoling to know that eight hundred years ago, Italy's reigning poet Dante was experiencing a mid-life crisis much like my own, though he put it a bit more eloquently than my "AARRGGGH!":

> *Midway upon the journey of our life*
> *I found myself within a forest dark,*
> *For the straightforward pathway had been lost.*
> *Ah, me! How hard a thing is to say,*
> *what was this forest savage, rough and stern,*
> *which in the very thought renews the fear.*
>
> *So bitter is it, death is little more...*

- The Divine Comedy

Fellow writer F. Scott Fitzgerald weighed in succinctly on the subject a few centuries later:

There are no second acts in American lives.

Fitzgerald shook the Minnesota dust off his heels early on and hobnobbed in Paris with the shining lights of the 1920's jazz age. He died at age forty-four, an alcoholic groping his way through his own "forest dark." I wonder what he observed in Europe that caused him to pinpoint such a telling difference in our cultures. What are Americans missing? In our quest for success, could we be leaving our inner desires behind? I used to think mid-life crises were the exclusive domain of balding men in red sports cars. I know now they are available to anyone who hits the halfway mark ignoring that little voice inside that keeps whispering, "Is this all there is?"

The first act in theatre generally ends with a predicament, or question, that requires resolution. The audience then stretches their legs at intermission, gets a glass of bubbly, maybe a breath of fresh air. They mingle in the lobby in the hopes of catching hold of something, a snatch of conversation or simply a twinkling trinket, that delights and inspires. Thus refreshed, they are ready to return to the theatre and witness the unfolding of the (hopefully skillful) solution.

My own first act came to a conclusion with the unexpected predicament of divorce. But even before things came to a head, I didn't look too far into the future, because all I could see was a flatline to the horizon. Good morning, good evening, and *good night.* Wash, rinse, repeat. Mortgage? Check. Kids? Check. Sports utility vehicle? Check. Dry mouth and itchy, watery heart? Check. I knew a flatline meant no pulse. Not good.

It was time for me to head out to the lobby, take a big gulp of air and start casting around for inspiration. My raw emotions, while painful, were actually a great internal guidance system. I had no extra energy to rationalize or navigate around them, so I just accepted them. And they led me back to the solace and joy of music. I realized that I had all but stopped listening to music because either my husband didn't like my taste, or the vibe was too dark for my young ones. But music had been my best friend since puberty. Back then, when my two-year-old brother Gordon would visit my little attic bedroom hideaway, I would teach him the names of the Stones from their album cover photos. Mick, Keith, Bill, Charlie, Brian... dear friends all. That bumper sticker that says *Books Save Lives*? So do record albums. I began my writing career literally five days after seeing the Cure play an unforgettable three-hour concert and feeling like they had blown the top of my head wide open.

During my divorce, I applied directly to my heart the balm of the Cure, the Sundays, David Bowie, Nick Drake, Cocteau Twins, Amp, the Smiths, Sheila Chandra and Chopin. They all said the same thing to me: *We know, we know how you feel, we've felt that way too, don't worry, it gets better.* Oftentimes, I was in the fetal position, unconsciously laboring away at a new birth. And then I started PLAYING music. And they were right... the second act gets better, it gets a lot better! No more flatlines - a hairpin turn here and there, to be sure, but past the forest dark there are rolling hills and even mountains, with spectacular scenic overlooks, and a sunset to die for.

How To Get Gigs
by Kristin

In the beginning of our Violet adventure, the girls and I longingly watched other bands out at clubs, curious about everything. How did they work together? How many sets did they perform? How did they get the gig in the first place? One day, I realized that I could talk to the band members that I personally know. Once I started, I became ruthless, I will say anything and ask any questions, no longer caring if I look like an idiot. Sometimes you have to put on your big girl panties and just get out there!

My husband hangs out with a band called Sideways Reign. They play at the restaurant where he works, performing every few months. After one of their shows, I approached the lead singer, Justin Stang, and told him about our Violet vision. I kept it short, but showed enthusiasm (and wasn't too tipsy!). Quite unexpectedly, he told us when we were ready we were welcome to open for them. It will be awhile before that happens, but to have that kind of affirmation from a fellow performer put a fire under me.

Another new band that is comprised of friends of mine, has also been an inspiration. Ten Cents in Oklahoma is their name and they will play anywhere: coffee shops, house parties, on boats, even in the parking lot of our local deli. One hot summer day, I had six kids with me and a Corona in hand. *And* a desire to dance. It was the antique car show/flea market and despite the heat (95 degrees), everyone had an upbeat attitude while the band pumped out song after song.

I noticed they were not drinking water, although beer cans and bottles littered the floor around them. The lead singer was sweating profusely and looked like she might faint dead away. I rushed into the deli and brought them a pitcher of water. They noticed my effort and after the show announced that I was their new "band mom." I'll take it! Approaching them afterward and telling them about our little threesome called Violet was easy. We all decided that we would be a perfect opener for them when we got our chops. Sweet ass deal!

Rain has written a few songs and they are sooo full of life. I was thinking about them when I went to see an old friend play recently at our new hangout in Olympia, a cafe/bar called Le Voyeur. After the angsty show, I asked the front woman if she would consider looking at one of Rain's songs, as it seems well suited for their band. She agreed, with genuine enthusiasm.

I know I am putting the red carpet before the film reel, the solo before the intro, but I also know practicing our craft, all of it, including finding out where to play (once we can play), is part of the process.

Hero Takes A Fall
by Rain

"Da DAH da da, da DAH da da... sing it! You know the song better than I do. That's the trouble with drummers. They don't sing." This from my drumming teacher Darlene, who was dancing around the room, trying to teach me the drum line to The Charlatan UK's "Jesus Hairdo." They are one of my favorite bands, each album an aural landscape of stellar songwriting, brisk execution and huge dollops of heart and soul.

It's the fourth song Darlene's taught me to pick apart. We started with "I Want To Hold Your Hand" by the Beatles and "Back On The Chain Gang" by the Pretenders. Luckily the band scratched "One Way Or Another" by Blondie, because that one was hellishly fast.

"Jesus Hairdo" is plenty quick, and tricky too. Jon Brookes, The Charlatans UK's drummer, performed at the World's Greatest Drummer Concert in 2009. Right *before* he had shoulder surgery. The man's a machine. All these wizened jazz greats, and there was strapping, long-haired Jon. Someone (his wife?) had manhandled him out of his usual skull t-shirt and stuffed him into a suit jacket.

"Try this," Darlene says, simplifying the beat.

"No," I insist. "I want to do what he's doing (I'll have what he's having)."

Jon started out performing in a jazz trio at his parents' pub. He's phenomenally inventive. He's been with The Charlatans UK for twenty years now, an amazing run of creativity, not to mention successful avoidance of Band Ego Implosion.

Last fall I spent hours composing a love letter to him, when he was in the hospital recovering from a brain tumor operation (at age forty-two). He collapsed during a concert, five days before I was set to see the band play for the first time. Crushing me. I had planned to travel two states over, my first airplane trip in five years and I already had the tickets.

Here's my letter:

> Jon, peace to you during your inward journey and recovery. You are the reason I am the drummer in a band. I have tons more to learn from you, so please hurry, get well and scheme up more diabolically propulsive rhythms for me to wrap my head around. Thank you for countless hours of unadulterated, STD-free pleasure. Love to you and the rest of the lads. Please please please re-schedule the US tour... we're parched for Charlification here on the west coast... we're pining...
>
> p.s. Happy late birthday!

The news became even scarier. Jon was suffering from Stage 4 cancer. For weeks I set aside time to meditate on him, seeing him enveloped in a golden healing light, and I know many others did the same. In the meantime, I learned more about my drumming hero. He's a big bruiser of a guy, solid, and I pictured him with a little rugby team of burly sons, so I was somewhat taken aback to find out he has three small girls... named after flowers. People endlessly surprise me.

Not a week out of surgery, Jon delighted his fans with a long, detailed summary of his experience. In it, he included these inspiring words:

> "I want to try and explain to anyone who is interested, the amazing power of 'positive thought' and love and light, which can be transmitted across vast amounts of time and space by everyone who wishes to try. I began to feel a portal open up inside my soul, and a feeling of well-being charge through me..."

About two months later, I received this thrilling update, The Charlatans UK website announced Jon returned to the stage and played at the band's New Year's Eve show in Edinburgh. He wrote on the site's forum: "Thanks for all the love, light, prayers and positive messages... just had results from my blood, brain and body scans... the cancer has gone!!! BIG LOVE... JB"

Big Love right back at ya, Jon.

Think Globally, Rock Locally
by Deborah

The local Olympia music scene has been a big influence on our Violet journey. For Rain, it started when she was despondent that she couldn't see her favorite band, The Charlatans UK playing in San Francisco when they had to halt their tour as their drummer, Jon, had a brain tumor. After a day of crying, she picked herself up and ventured to downtown Olympia where she stumbled across The Missionary Position.

I had already enjoyed a band called Deadwood Revival, again a stumble. Their fiddler's story is worth a mention - she had watched the band for years and finally got the courage to expand her violin playing at age forty-two, when her eighty-two-year-old grandmother told her to follow her dreams, as she was "still a spring chicken." A year later she had joined the band she faithfully followed.

We have discovered that Olympia has quite an eclectic and prodigious music scene. The bands cover the gamut, from bluegrass to punk. Although I must confess, the acts that Olympia is known for nationally - grunge groups like Nirvana, are completely lost on me (those are Rain's reviews to write...).

Not every show in Oly is well attended, even at the small clubs, which provides an intimacy we enjoy. As far as the venues go, there is Le Voyeur, a trippy back room as big as a coat closet, the Eastside, home to the most hippy grooves, and the Fourth Ave Tavern. The last two joints have popular pool tables, which bands compete with for the patrons' attention. There is also

Ben Moore's, the oldest bar in town, dating back to the 1800s, where Skyler's band, Sour Owl, often plays. We even have a big-time theatre, The Capitol, a glamorous old broad, always in need of fundraising, where we recently saw The Gossip perform. Their powerhouse vocalist, Beth Ditto, once served lattes right here in Olympia. No time for that now, as the Gossip are favorites on the European concert circuit.

Not that global rock concerts are difficult to find in the Northwest - a quick foray to Seattle or Portland and you can pretty much catch anyone eventually. Joan Baez, Martin Sexton and Michael Franti are headliners we have sought out. Twenty minutes away at the Tacoma Dome, any pop star you are willing to throw $150 at can be had - this year alone, Lady Gaga and Justin Beiber sold out concerts. And for those over a certain age, there are the casinos, where this month, Smokey Robinson, Air Supply and Three Dog Night are crooning.

Of course, we would love to go to more big ticket concerts, but our budgets limit us to peanut butter and music lessons for our kids, so we thank god for YouTube and iTunes, where we check out our favorite rock stars, and for the small shows in our backyard. Unlike the show stoppers, here, we are able to talk to musicians between sets, see how they interact with one another and if the lead singer needs to get her roots done, all the things you don't see on the huge stage. We just hope our local musicians are getting at least half of that four dollar cover.

Viva Las Vegas
by Rain

Deborah and I put on our writing caps the other night and stepped out to an author reading at Swing, a swank wine bar in Olympia. Deborah herself has braved the podium, offering poems from her book *The Mother Ship*, and beautifully, too, I might add. The wine bar basement, twinkle lights aglow, filled up rapidly with a new crowd for me, slightly hipster, slightly yuppie, slightly... buzzed.

This time the stage was taken by Viva Las Vegas, a Portland stripper, musician and sex worker activist. Dressed in muted slacks and t-shirt, wearing little makeup, she seemed cast refreshingly against type. Not so much as a pastie in sight. Her bio states she matriculated from a top-drawer college, and she trains a steady, anthropologist's eye on her subjects. To top it all off, she's a preacher's daughter.

Viva took a stiff slug from her margarita and plunged in. She read from a selection of essays, her style a marriage of wry humor, abundant heart and a touch of indignation. One hilarious piece described how she was punched by an obstreperous customer, punched him right back, and became the heroine of the strip club, resulting in tips and drinks all round and the lasting tang of empowerment. She makes an excellent case for stripping as a legitimate art, one in which women are in full entrepreneurial charge of their bodies and livelihoods.

Viva writes how her large, hated, Norwegian ass had followed her around all her life, but that it wasn't until she became a stripper, that she realized her ass was an ass-et!

A poignant, honest essay related her journey through the less-than-sensitive labyrinth of breast cancer care. Yes, she still strips once a week, if only to reclaim her sexuality after a mastectomy. "And I like to share my smile," she reflected. "A smile is a very powerful thing." A smile, she makes clear in her memoir *Magic Gardens,* that doesn't always make it home, once she wipes off all the glitter and lipstick and faces her old foe, depression. What creative artist can't relate to that?

Afterwards, I approached her table, where she sat with her quiet, cuddly partner. I felt an immediate kinship with her. In addition to stripping and writing, Viva also fronts two bands, Coco Cobra and the Killers (punk), and The Lesser Saints (americana).

"I feel like I could've been you, if I hadn't married and had children," I began. "Except for the taking-your-clothes-off-in-public part."

"Well, it looks good on you!" she replied.

Here's to Viva. As she states in her book, she had committed the greatest crime a woman can commit in our society by claiming her right to her own sexuality. Women like Viva, living balls-out, as it were, on the front lines, make it easier for the rest of us to explore ourselves, even if only in private.

Muses and Managers
by Kristin

Skyler is officially my music teacher, but there are a few other groove gurus in my life - foremost, my seven-year-old son, Coletrane. My husband and I gave him his name because we had a feeling that he would create his own genius and lo and behold, this star child has a passion for music just like his mama and his namesake. When I tell people his name, they audibly gasp. Let's face it, John Coltrane was the man. My Cole is not only inspired, he is a taskmaster, when I am feeling lazy he yells, "Mama, are you kidding!! We need to get this song down, let's go through it a few more times. Come on, let's do this!"

When we were on our way to Violet's first gig, I, grasping the steering wheel with anxiety, looked in the rear view mirror and saw Cole mouthing the words to the song we were about to perform. His eyes met mine and he said, " Mom, my favorite band is Violet." Silent tears came down my cheek and I knew he would be there for me through my music journey. When I feel like I need a little inspiration, he is my guy.

Recently, Deborah shared a theory that children choose the parents that are right for them. She explained that one could say Mozart became who he was because he had musical parents, but another thought is that Mozart chose musical parents because he wanted to make great music and knew he needed the environment they could offer. I believe Cole chose me because he knew in his soul, that I would allow him to discover and develop his natural abilities to entertain. I am the perfect stage mom, and being in a band at my age is showing Cole that you can do and be anything anytime.

In terms of being sensitive and expressive, Cole has been given gifts from his grandparents as well. I have always been a gregarious soul, something I inherited and learned from my own parents. Although my Mom is not going to perform anytime soon, she is supportive and kind to everyone. She loves me in ways that no one else can, with warmth and just the right words.

Dad? Well, let's just say that since age two, I have heard him sing the same Neil Young songs and his anthem, "Lucy in the Sky With Diamonds." I am his Lucy. My father has played the guitar on and off for thirty years. Matter-of-fact, I hooked him up with our teacher Skyler so that he can finally realize his dream of having his own band, performing songs that he has written. He just finished one and proudly performed last weekend at his first open mic. I love jamming with him because as he says, "Kristin, people love seeing a daughter and her dad singing together!" He hounds me about practicing and leads me through creative visualizations that help relax me. My dad and I both have ADD, which is a challenge, but because of his support and encouragement, I see myself on the stage playing and singing at the same time, not an easy task.

Cole and I jammed out to Lucinda Williams yesterday over and over, until I had the song memorized, and now it is in my muscle memory. I would not be able to do this without familial support.

Viva's Vapor Trail
by Rain

Deborah and I went to Portland, Oregon last night on what turned out to be a wild goose chase, but an entertaining one. We had hoped to see stripper/writer/musician Viva Las Vegas perform with her new band, The Lesser Saints, but no luck. Something got lost in translation. We'd been directed to the posh Bunk Bar, which was full of interesting-looking over-thirties, talking nineteen to a dozen; there wasn't even any music playing for atmosphere, didn't need it. Everyone at the Bunk Bar seemed to know Viva, and eagerly gave us directions to Mary's Strip Club, where Viva strips. When we got there, we discovered we were too late for her gig, which had been at a different venue altogether. Sigh.

We stayed for a drink and our first peek at a strip show, which in Portland is fully nude. This was not at all like the house of mirrors, assembly line strip clubs in the movies. The club managed to be all at once, welcoming, edgy, slightly seamy, and just a little sad (it was a Monday night, after all). A sprinkling of men stared quietly. The women bartenders were motherly. The jukebox rocked - I recognized a Cake tune and was impressed, thinking Portland's baseline level of culture seems higher than most. Even in a strip club.

One girl was tattooed and bored, the other perky and playful, and both were friendly to us offstage. Both wore wigs. And bikinis, which didn't take long to shed. I wished for a little more delay of gratification, a little more of a performance. Interesting to note both girls were fully shaved, and thankfully,

70

had no artificial body parts. They also made no attempt to suck in their tummies, a revelation to these Violets who came of age in the Jane Fonda workout years.

I'd go back. It made me feel kind of sexy, like, yeah, I've got one of those and two of those and, yeah, they *are* pretty cute.

A gentleman named Chris, who was the self-appointed club "Grand Poobah," left his stripper-massaging duties to take us somewhere we could dance. He deposited us a few blocks down at the flaming gates of a bar called Dante's to experience Karaoke from Hell, which turned out to be an amazing live band that fronted a succession of singers from the audience. They had a chick drummer and bassist! The crowd was lively and warm, and at one point we all swayed and sang "Time After Time" together (I think it was sometime after my third cosmo).

Deborah and I came up with lots of new ideas for the band and blog. We wound up eating slammin' street pizza and talking all the way home until (ouch) three a.m.

Flying Flamenco-Style
by Deborah

I like to think that life is not a crap shoot, it is not Russian Roulette, that there is purpose and meaning. I recently met drummer, Joey Heredia, and the experience was a cosmic YES. Yes, baby, you are on the right track, keep going.

Once a year, I go to my old stomping ground in Southern California for a mini-personal retreat. I lived in Santa Barbara for twelve years all told, grew from a seventeen-year-old college freshman to a mother with two young boys. Home was many places, from the student "ghetto" of Isla Vista (a ghetto with an ocean view and eighteen-year-olds driving BMWs), to the suburbs of Goleta, where my ex-husband and I had our first child, until we made it to the real deal of SB (as Santa Barbara is called). Finally, in our last move, we settled further south in a town of thirteen thousand, Carpinteria. When I go south now, I often do not make it to Santa Barbara, preferring the simplicity of the town that boasts, "home of the safest beach in California." Once in Cali, I do not write, I do not practice music, I walk on the beach and swim in the ocean, all the while yakking with one of my dearest girlfriends, Marla.

I usually fly into Santa Barbara itself (the airport is like a movie set) but this trip, because of cheaper tickets and the fact that Marla's dog was at her mom's house in LA, I chose Burbank. This was the first machination of the universe to get me to meet Joey. Here's where it got cosmic. I was late for my flight in Seattle and literally ran to the plane. I was huffy and stressed, one of the last people to approach the gate, where a hipster/

gangster wearing black leather and sunglasses sat and bemusedly watched me rush by. Once on the plane, I found a woman in my 25C seat looking out the window. She was confused and didn't speak English. I called the stewardess to facilitate a switch, but the woman seemed so bewildered, I gave up and reluctantly offered to take her place in the middle of the next row. A few moments later, the gangsta/artist/sunglass guy plunked down beside me and said, "Well, fancy that!"

Which was the beginning of a two hour meeting of the heart and mind, plus a lot of flamenco. Turned out Joey is a drummer, he had just performed with a band in Seattle (his saxophone player smiled at me from across the aisle). In a matter of five minutes I told him my whole story - mom, writer, poet, divorced, in love. Joey inhaled and offered to buy me breakfast. We both got the chorizo and eggs, the best airplane food either of us had ever tasted, which I washed down with a Bloody Mary. He wouldn't let me pay, said, "I have so much money I don't know what to do with it" and giggled. Me, being a student of abundance, queried him, to which he explained he has a beautiful life doing exactly what he has always loved, which is to play drums, and although he isn't wealthy, he is well-enough off, preferring a modest lifestyle.

Joey shared he is more a student than ever, even though he has accomplished all of his goals and played for very big names. He had recently discovered flamenco. He asked if he could show me a video aptly titled *Flamenco,* directed by Carlos Suarez, and proceeded to pull out a little DVD player. The movie is a series of vignettes, flamenco singing and dancing in various forms, all masterfully, yet sparsely directed, with beautiful sets and lighting. The first singer was a woman in her seventies who taught me more about emotion and longing and how to move an audience than any vocal teacher I have ever encountered. Her face contorted as her song, her saga continued. This matron showed me I do not have to be pretty or young or perfect to move others, I just need to feel. The DVD went on, each offering richer than the last. While Joey kept time on my forearm tapping the off-beats, I cried with the beauty of the expression.

We talked about love, art, his enthusiasm for Los Angeles, about how he was a true street kid from East LA, who by the odds should be dead or in jail. He began asking for a drum set when he was ten and was not given one until he was sixteen, as his mother's health began to falter and he coped by running with the wrong crowd. By grace he was connected with one of the granddads of drumming and has had an amazing life as a result. Flamenco is a turning of the wheel for him, his now deceased mother was a flamenco and jazz singer. Joey asked if I would like to stop by later that afternoon for a rehearsal, one of the finest flamenco singers in the world was coming. Later that evening we could go salsa dancing at a club that had been there for thirty years and lastly, check out Will Smith's new recording studio, which according to Joey, is the talk of the town and just across the alley.

Now, if Rain had been greeting me at baggage claim, it would have been a no-think, but my friend Marla had a lonely dog to contend with and her sights set on me, our toes in the sand and a bottle of wine. As did I. I parted with Joey after two hours which felt like two lifetimes, as if we had made both music and love. Joey saw my light, he saw my sparkly self. He proclaimed, "You are like a little girl who never grew up!" Easier to feel when I am on an airplane headed to the beach for three days, but I felt rekindled and grateful nonetheless.

FOLLOWING THE BEAT OF MY OWN DRUM
BY RAIN

Our debut is a week away, playing one whole song at the Rhythm Fire School of Rock quarterly concert. We are going to perform Lucinda Williams' alt-country song, "Can't Let Go." We especially love her because she is of a certain age and is still full of juice. The song is a challenge for me because there are no drums on the original track at all - nothing to copy. Our sensei, Skyler, started me out with the most basic rock beat, boom chick boom chick. After a while, that seemed kind of boring, and it would not impress any drummers in the audience! Which of course is my goal in life.

Many people seem wowed by what I call the "arsonist" approach to drumming. Fast, furious and noisy. Not me. I like impeccable. I like choice. I think discretion is the better part of drumming. The beat deliberately left out, which sets up anticipation, which catches you by surprise.

I think the best drum line I've learned so far has been on The Pretenders "Back On the Chain Gang." The verse beat is classic rock: boom chick, boom boom chick. But every time Martin Chambers goes into the chorus, the drum fill is slightly different. It comes in a beat late, or a beat early: one snare, one tom, one crash. But the next time: two snare, two tom, two snare, one crash. He throws in a little SNAP!, here and there, just to see if you're paying attention.

I listened to the Lucinda Williams track several times. It aches with heartbreak. The classic, stripped-down arrangement allows the lyrics and vocals to shine through. It's mostly about the guitars - at least three of them. I wanted to give it a propulsive beat to match the lyric about being broken down like a train wreck. That was it - the drums should sound like a locomotive barreling through the lonesome heartland. Like how it feels when your love turns into a runaway train.

I played around and eventually found what I thought would work. Boom boom chick, boom boom chick on the verse, with the hi-hat struck only every other beat to let the spareness of the song come through. Then, kicking into the chorus, faster, boom chick boom chick, with the hi-hat going double time. Skyler said the guitar solo is usually accompanied by the same beat as the chorus, but that sounds too fast to me. So I play the verse part, boom boom chick, but double up on the hi-hat to keep the tension up.

This may all sound like hornswaddle to any seasoned drummers out there, and if so, I apologize. I am feeling my way here, which is kind of like roller skating without underpants. Teaching myself, I may end up with serious road rash. But, what a way to go!

Country Weak
by Deborah

Sometimes a movie is just entertainment, sometimes it is a full-blown testament to the fallacy of Hollywood stereotypes. My movie night with Rain began well enough - a perfect girl date, with snuck-in organic popcorn and fair trade chocolate, preceded by two cosmos at the pizza joint/bar next door. We were primed to be inspired.

Country Strong is the tragic story of an almost washed-up country singer, Kelly Canter (played by Gwyneth Paltrow), who has serious addiction issues. She and her husband/manager, James Canter (played by Tim McGraw, the famous country singer) have a tumultuous marriage which may or may not have exacerbated her addiction. The other main characters are two up-and-coming young country stars who open for Kelly Canter.

In short, the theme of the movie is that you can't have both fame and love. Spoiler Alert! Gwyneth spells this out the night before her big comeback after completing rehab, advising her opening act with just those words. She then kills herself after the concert with an overdose of pills while her entourage is waiting to congratulate her. In the final scene, the male upstart is back in his small town singing to a dozen people at a small bar, where he is joined by the young starlet who decides not to follow her career, but to be with her man. Gone are the Stetsons and the eyeliner.

Rain and I practically threw our popcorn kernels at the screen.

Two things enraged us about this movie. Rain's particular bone to pick was that women are so rarely allowed a second act in our culture. Kelly, who is "aging out," is not shown becoming a grand dame of music, not allowed to retire from the industry and find another meaningful career, not allowed to mentor the young upstart, who in the movie is merely competition.

The themes of addiction and stardom are common, because so many of our divas and actresses battle such demons and destruction. While too many do culminate in a tragic death, many come through such challenges stronger and wiser, singers such as Bonnie Raitt and Belinda Carlisle (of the Go-Gos). There are also many women to emulate who never went down that road in the first place, from Joan Baez to Beyoncé.

My contention was more with the theme itself, that love and fame cannot co-exist. I am thinking of some of the musicians I most admire: Bono from U2, Sting, Pat Benatar, Paul McCartney, all who had or have long-term marriages. The irony with *Country Strong* is that the two main actors themselves have marriages which seem to endure the strains of stardom. Tim McGraw is famously married to Faith Hill, raising their three girls on the road and a farm in Nashville, while Gwyneth Paltrow is wed to Chris Martin (lead singer of the band Coldplay) with two children. In a pre-movie interview, Paltrow gushed about how her family had vaca-tioned with the Hill-McGraw clan down south and the strong friendship bonds that were forged.

We were upset that fame (which happens as the result of following one's passion) was depicted as being a kiss of death, literally or figuratively. We hunger for stories where women live happily ever after, pursuing their dreams of love and expression.

Does anyone remember Isabella Rossellini? The daughter of filmmaker, Ingrid Bergman, she was one of the first models to secure tenure as the face of Lancôme for fourteen years. She acted in artsy films such as *Blue Velvet* and appeared at the age of thirty-six in Madonna's controversial book, *Sex*. Her second act is one of my favorites - she wrote and co-directed two-minute short films about the mating lives of insects, called *Green Porno*.

Rather than the disappointing ending of *Country Strong,* I would have much preferred to watch a reality show about the real life of Gwyneth, who juggles children and a career, manages to stay married to a partner who also has pursued his dreams. As of late, in addition to her acting, she has published a cookbook of healthy eating, hosts an active blog called *goop* where she shares her favorites goodies and bravely continues her singing career, appearing as a regular guest on the popular show, *Glee*. Gwyneth is a perfect example of an evolving artist. Perhaps she should try her hand at script writing.

THE THREE STOOGES PLAY THEIR FIRST GIG EVER
BY RAIN

Two hours before showtime, Larry, Moe and Curly, aka Deborah, Kristin and myself, were engaged in various preparatory activities across town. Deborah was wetting her whistle on half a beer at the Eastside Tavern after sobbing on her beau's shoulder and smearing all of her carefully-applied stage makeup. Kristin was gathering the confetti of socks, shoes, coats and children. I was caging cigarettes off old friends at the Brotherhood Lounge while steadfastly refusing to reveal the location of our first gig.

"Come next time," I urged. "Come when we know *two* songs." The thought of anyone I knew being there only made me twice as nauseous.

Violet the band met up at nine p.m. in the parking lot of the Black Lake Grange. It was right next door to the fire station, so burly firefighters were on hand if, God forbid, we stubbed a finger or expired from fright. As we swigged from Deborah's organic energy drink, we admired each other's outfits: Deborah in sexy jeans and purple swing t-shirt, me in a flirty violet minidress and leggings. Kristin's wooly knee highs paired with her new black buckled platforms won highest marks. Luckily, I had given her a lesson earlier on how to walk in heels. "Tuck your booty in, keep your knees together, shoulders down, and work it, girl!"

The Grange was stuffed with friends and family members of the Rhythm Fire kids, who were rockin' out with serious attitude. We slouched on a bench in the back and muttered to each other.

"Crap. They're really good."
"Some of them play multiple instruments *while* they are singing."
"Crap."

Darlene, my drumming teacher, wandered over and picked up a wilting tinsel and wire centerpiece. "We could only afford one table decoration, so we're moving it around," she joked. Using our mind-control superpowers, which are an essential tool for any band, we willed the people around us to leave. "Go! Go now. Vamanos. Nah nah nah, goooooodbye!" And little by little, they trickled out, as their spawn finished playing.

An hour later, Darlene happened over again. She looked torn. "It's getting pretty late, I've been here since five," she hinted.

"Oh, you should go home. Definitely. We know you'll be here in spirit!" we chirped. So she, too, left. Phew. One less witness to the execution.

"We are going to make a mint, not telling anyone where we're playing and hoping everyone flees," I noted.
"No doubt," Deborah concurred.
We couldn't see Kristin because she was buried under her two exhausted boys, but we think we heard her say "Yup." Or maybe it was "Help."

10:45 p.m. Finally, it was our turn. The stage was a giant lego board of amps and monitors, with cables snaking across the floor. Treacherous, especially when your knees are knocking together. I focused on switching the drums around to accommodate my left-handedness and avoided looking at the sparse audience, who were most definitely not in the dark, as I had been led to believe. Skyler was there to play lead guitar with us and lend moral support.

Deborah made a short speech introducing us. "We're called Violet, our kids go to Rhythm Fire, and they have so much fun, we thought we'd try it as well. We've been playing together for a couple of months, so be gentle with us!" she shared humbly. It was my job to start things off. I looked at Kristin at the keyboard, maracas and high-wattage smile at the ready, and at Deborah with her electric guitar and even more electric ass. My eyes dropped to my trusty metronome and held on for dear life. "ONE, TWO, ONE TWO THREE FOUR!" I shouted and we were off. It was exactly how I imagine riding a dragon would be.

As I banged away, I thought how odd it felt to be behind my bandmates. In rehearsal we sit in a tight-knit circle. The music feels like magic we coax forth from a cauldron between us. Now all I saw were the backs of my fellow band members. Instead of music, I just heard drums. Deborah and Kristin's voices were faint, I imagine because the speakers faced the audience. Our perspective had radically shifted; we were facing outward, not inward. I learned quickly that performing and simply playing are two very different animals.

84

We got off track at one point, but Skyler shouted "Chorus on four!" and we got back on without too much drama. It was over in three minutes and the crowd went WILD!! They cheered, they stood on their seats, they stomped... just kidding. Everyone applauded the brave moms, but I couldn't help wondering, did it even sound like music? I hoped so. Before we headed out to unwind with a drink and some dancing, Skyler came up to us.

"Mad respect to you guys for getting on stage and playing... it was great!"
"We messed up!" we lamented.
"That happens to everyone, and we'll talk about what to do when that happens at our next rehearsal. But, do you feel ALIVE?"

That we did.

Smack a Smile on Your Face and It's All Good
by Kristin

As I drove to Violet's first performance, I pulled up my over-the-knee socks and adjusted my stiletto on the gas pedal. I took a gulp of air and said my mantra, "It is only one song, we can pull off one song."

Rain texted as I approached the fire station which was next door to the club. Okay, it wasn't exactly a night club, but more of a grange. I scanned her text as I pulled the key out of the ignition. It read: "Gulp, a case of the nerves." Oh man. My boys were in the backseat wide-eyed with anticipation. My oldest son, Coletrane, read my energy, as is his habit and said, "You look great, mama, when you see me in the audience I will give you a thumbs up!" Somehow I made it out of the car.

I brought the boys to my dad who was sitting alongside his open mike buddy Brandon. I love hanging out with Brandon at my dad's favorite bar on Thursday nights. We always get stoked when someone belts out a karaoke eighties rock number. He has seen me jump on stage and do backup vocals for our friends. He witnessed me affirming that one day I would be part of a band. And here he was, front and center.

As soon as my boys started playing with grandpa, Violet was out of there. We beelined to Deb's minivan and I showed them my skanty knickers! I had a sexy, sequined, black top on, but to take the seriousness out of it, I wore my favorite pair of little polka dot boy shorts that have seen the inside of the washing machine a few too many times. We had a good laugh and munched on chips as we perfected our game plan, which was to visualize almost everyone leaving the grange.

The groups before us were teenagers and they were smokin' hot. They also knew more than one song! The place was packed so we sat on top of one another on a bench along a wall. We waited two-and-a-half hours to go on, two-and-a-half hours past my boys' bedtimes. Azure and Coletrane were fading, but I hoped they might remember this night for a very long time. I had one boy on each knee and tried to maintain my rock star look. Not so easy with a three-year-old's hand down my shirt. The knee socks were sagging and I was beginning to sweat. Thankfully my dad took the both of them and tossed them about while I got it together in the bathroom. The clock struck eleven. We were on.

We were announced as the "adult group." I died laughing. As we shuffled up the stage stairs I remembered what Rain taught me, keep your knees together, tuck your tailbone in and walk. My first pair of heels and I was gonna rock' em. We were not in our usual positions on stage and Deb and I exchanged a look like, "Oh, wow, we are so majorly out of our comfort zone."

We launched into our song, only to find that the keyboard was cutting out. Skyler stopped us mid-way through the first verse to fix the problem. He said he wanted us set up for success. Nice wish. I stood there with a shaker in one hand and played the keyboard with my other. I looked out at our audience and saw smiling people. Coletrane was on my dad's shoulders beaming. My smile never faded. Not even when we screwed up and Skyler shouted, "Go back to the chorus, Violet!"

We did, and then we exited the stage. Shaky knees and all, I knew that this was where I belonged.

Sappy Love Songs
by Deborah

I have been singing with Mark, my vocal teacher and founder of Rhythm Fire, for a few months now and we've just learned we both like sappy duets. Really sappy ones. The movie trailer kind. During one of our vocal lessons, we spent half of our time googling Joe Cocker, Dolly Parton, Marvin Gaye and more. We decided to pick a few to work on for an upcoming Rhythm Fire gig. We chose "Cruisin," the Huey Lewis and Gwyneth Paltrow version, and "What Kind of Fool" by Barbra Streisand and Barry Gibb. Singing Streisand was a multi-layered journey for me, I elaborate in the following pages, but for now, I want to focus on what it was like to sing with Mark.

I am shy. Mark is not, he fills an arena when he sings. His work with me has been getting me to open my mouth and sing loudly from my body, from my soul. Making eye contact with another person while singing was also new for me. Even though we were basically doing what any decent karaoke duo does, it was a challenge for me to:

1. sing
2. remember the lyrics
3. make eye contact with Mark and most surprisingly
4. not notice how cute Mark is

Ahhh... the gist here of my writing. Beware of singing love songs! I now have an appreciation of how movie actors and stage performers end up together. There is a certain chemistry generated when working on something, especially something as heart opening as singing a love song. I care about Mark like a brother and have from the start, so it was weird to have a sudden wave of "Wow!" I also have met Mark's amazing wife, Betsy, and was blown away by how lovely and juicy she is. Needless, to say, I did not pursue any feelings generated when we were crooning about "opening up" and "going inside." We laughed it off, slugged each other on the arm and kept singing. All in a day's work!

We never did get to perform "Cruisin'" at the end of the Rhythm Fire show, but I'm hooked. I am working on "Baby, It's Cold Outside" for the holidays, with whoever is willing to sing it with me (I've even printed up the lyrics so they have no excuse not to!). Here are a few of the most popular love duets:

House of Love - Amy Grant and Vince Gill
Up Where We Belong - Joe Cocker and Jennifer Warnes
Cruisin' - Huey Lewis and Gwyneth Paltrow
It's Your Love - Tim McGraw and Faith Hill
Don't Go Breaking My Heart - Elton John and Kiki Dee
You've Got a Friend - Roberta Flack and Donny Hathaway
Ain't Nothing Like the Real Thing -
Marvin Gaye and Tammi Terell
Tonight, I Celebrate My Love -
Peabo Bryson and Roberta Flack
Islands in the Stream - Dolly Parton and Kenny Rogers
(Just) You and I - Eddie Rabbitt and Crystal Gayle
Endless Love - Diana Ross and Lionel Ritchie

Bringing Back Barbra
by Deborah

As a young teen, holed up in my yellow bedroom, alone or with friends, I listened to Barbra Streisand's albums obsessively. Amazing to discover, thirty years later, that I would find one song in particular, "What Kind of Fool" sung by Barbra and Barry Gibb, to be completely cathartic. Mark and I were picking out duets and came upon the duo hashing out heartbreak in a video produced in the seventies. Barbra looks dated in white pumps and pantyhose. Barry, however, tops her with skintight pants, a blouse open exposing his hairy chest, and feathered hair, lacquered in place.

Having experienced infidelity in my past, the lyrics cut deeply, and singing them with Mark was better therapy than hours in the counseling chair. While I can't quote the lyrics here (those *&%#$! music lawyers!), I can tell you the woman talks about the man letting "the stranger" in.

Now, I do think ultimately my past relationships ended for the better, absolutely. However, I wouldn't want to experience that betrayal again. At one point when Barbra gets really uppity, I felt heat surge through my body. The song has a large vocal range and taps the emotional range as well, the bittersweetness of knowing something is irrevocably broken, yet still having tremendous love for the other person.

As a girl, I listened to the album *Guilty* (which featured "What Kind of Fool") and Barbra's other ballad-infused LP, *A Star Is Born*, over and over. The lines from "You Don't Bring Me

Flowers" when she mentions the man not bringing flowers or singing love songs, and he bemoans that she doesn't come to the door anymore when he returns at the end of a long day described my parents' marriage and subsequent divorce.

Barbra Streisand touched generations, she is still considered one of, if not the best, female vocalists of all time.

Here is a poem I wrote called "Evergreen" about my adolescence comforted by Barbra:

Evergreen

The morning after my father's death,
my sister and I took turns napping in the cargo area
of the old station wagon, nestled in blankets.
I remember my mother and her new husband's
hushed and urgent voices the six hundred miles
from Sacramento to San Diego,
where I had just lived with my dad for the past year,
his request in the custody settlement.
It was a Friday, I being almost thirteen,
already taking comfort from food,
had whipped up a chocolate chip
Snackin' Cake to take with us,
let it bake while we quickly packed.

We returned Sunday night
to find the oven hot and angry,
I'd left it on the whole weekend,
felt ashamed to face my new step dad,

who was an energy consultant.
It was 1979 and people were waiting in line
at the gas station,
I was already trained to close windows
before the house warmed.

Back in school on Monday,
I felt bewildered overhearing the comments the kids made,
"I wouldn't be here so soon if my dad had died."
I began to look for solace, not in my mother's arms
but in my peers and the pubescent boys
who had begun to notice my budding body.

Years later in therapy, when faced with
what felt like the death of a relationship,
I was asked what got me through those times
and I remembered Barbra Streisand
and her hit album, *A Star Is Born.*
My girlfriends and I would sit on my bed and sing,
tears streaming down our faces,
lamenting the broken-hearted ballad of
Streisand and Kristofferson.
My only friend whose parents
weren't divorced or divorcing
had a cruel father, she hoped he would leave.
"You Don't Bring Me Flowers" was our anthem and
as soon as the song ended,
we'd move the needle back into the worn groove.

It was the song "Evergreen"
and the land that surrounded our home,
the biggest house I'd ever lived in, that offered comfort.
I had my own bedroom
with a built-in desk and cupboards,
a low window adolescent boys
would crawl in and out of.
I walked the trails that surrounded our house
and threw my cigarette butts in silty soil,
where the oaks, if you could call them evergreens,
were shallowly rooted,
their canopies brittle and full
against the Sacramento sky.

WILL SING FOR FOOD
BY RAIN

I've been listening to Blind Melon again. I remember playing their first album nonstop in the mid-nineties when I was working at a small gym in Spain. Every month, I was budgeted to purchase one new CD. It was my favorite job duty (collecting sweaty towels being distinctly lower on the list), and no Olympic judge ever made their selection with more care than I. Blind Melon's meticulous guitar rock was a welcome throwback to 70's bands like Led Zeppelin, in an era riddled with showy boy bands.

Blind Melon's monster hit was "No Rain." Their video featured a chubby, tap-dancing girl in glasses and a bee costume. She gets laughed at until she opens a gate to a sunny field full of fellow bee dancers. My heart still soars every time she pushes open the iron bars, a look of incredulous delight on her face.

As a fledgling musician, I see the Blind Melon concert footage and interviews in a fresh light. The overgrown haircuts, bagged-out t-shirts and bare feet form an aesthetic that succinctly states *starving artist*. When the band posed nude on the cover of *Rolling Stone*, I bet it was because their one outfit was at the laundromat.

I encounter these types all over downtown Olympia, every barista has a band, every dishwasher is working on his art. I love it. I am struck anew with the knowledge that Kurt Cobain wrote "Smells Like Teen Spirit" in a $137/month apartment here that he couldn't afford, and was evicted from. Interestingly, when Cobain was interviewed after his massive success with Nirvana, he admitted that shopping at thrift stores for odd treasures was not as much fun once he could buy out the entire store.

I am currently searching for a job, and my over-riding concern is that it doesn't take too much time away from my main loves: my children, my music and my writing. How to keep a roof overhead and shoes underfoot while following your muse is a tricky one.

My new favorite video of Blind Melon's, "Tones of Home, " is helping me along. Interwoven with footage of the band seriously rocking out are shots of a skinny, older woman in a Depression-era dress. She stands on hard-packed earth next to a rickety country house. The color is washed-out, but there is nothing pale about her passion. She sings along to the track, raising her voice to the heavens, shimmying and jigging her heart out.

On a Guitar String
by Deborah

The other day, as I went to open Rain's fridge, she warned, "There's only a leek and a beet in there!" I, who had just written a check at Safeway instead of using my debit card because payday was still two days away, completely understood (Rain informed me this practice is illegal, there is actually a term for it - *kiting*).

We have been trying to do Violet on the cheap, hopefully following in the footsteps of most rags to riches stories. Here the riches being the satisfaction of accomplishing our dreams (oh, sure we'd also like a best-selling book and the movie rights). In the long tradition of hungry musicians, we remember that the Beatles learned to harmonize because their car had no heating and they had to snuggle up to keep warm, singing to pass the cold England journeys. We invoke the rock goddess, Jewel, who was famously homeless in Alaska, as well as stars such as Celine Dion, Shania Twain and Jay-Z, who all came from hardscrabble beginnings.

Speaking of rags, our rock apparel is usually "vintage," aka thrift store with a 30% off coupon, although we do splurge rarely at Ross or Marshall's for the occasional clearance rack find. We figure because we are old and wise, we are bypassing the whole addiction thing, saving on both drugs and costly rehabs (they say it takes on average, six times to finally get clean). Plus being older and wiser, we are not engaging in scandalous behaviors which the paparazzi or journalists care about, thus saving on any lawsuits, no crotch shots for us.

Rain got a drum set for a couple hundred dollars off craigslist, I am playing the electric guitar that I inherited from my son when he upgraded at age fifteen. We spend money basically on two things - music lessons and Band Research (aka drinking and listening to music). Even then we have become more penurious, preferring happy hour or staying in curled up on my bed to nights on the town.

Our tab? Violet music lessons twice a month add up to $120 and I am taking guitar and vocal lessons every other week, for a total of $130. That's $250 a month hard costs for the months we actually schedule lessons, which is about half the time. With Vista Print, we knocked out business cards for ten dollars and GoDaddy hosts our website, $40 a year. Throw in a few iTunes downloads we'd most likely buy anyway. As to happy hour, we'd go even without the Violet excuse.

We feel supremely blessed to have the funds and time (time? what time?) to learn our instruments, they are hard won on both counts.

"I Hugged Bella Thorne"
by Rain

The line snaked around, past the small stage outside of Macy's, all the way into the center of the mall. Entire families, sprinkled with pubescent girls, waited patiently. The savviest brought camp chairs. I brought a book.

"Mom, it's Bella Thorne, the star of *Shake It Up*," my eleven-year-old daughter Gemma exulted. "She's the next Hannah Montana! It's like you meeting Nirvana."
"He's dead," her friend Talia chimed in.
"Well, okay - the Beatles, then," Gemma continued.
"Also dead. Most of them, anyway," interjected Talia help-fully.
"So, it's like me meeting Tori Amos," I offered.
"Who?" they chorused. I gave up.

My daughter and her three friends were resplendent in tutus, knee-high Converse sneakers and neon hair bows. I followed behind like a pack mule with snacks for the weary wait. As I looked around, I had an 80's flashback moment. Where was Cyndi Lauper when I needed her? Probably further back in line, with her own tweenager. It was the hottest day of the summer in Seattle, a crippling 85 degrees. But these girls were interested in a different kind of heat, the one that beams off a star. Would Bella's sparkle dust rub off on them? She certainly inspired them enough to break out into spontaneous song and dance in the aisles.

After three hours of waiting, a loudspeaker finally blared: "Put your hands together for BELLA THORNE!" A shrill scream rose from the crowd, a sound only young girls or a pack of starving hyenas could make. Bella came dancing into the mall, with five handlers trailing behind. She pranced onto the stage, popping and locking her little thirteen-year-old heart out. Then she sat down and began autographing photographs at the speed of light.

"Dude, she's actually talking to people!" Talia chirped. We shuffled forward like penitents at Lourdes. To one side of Bella stood a twenty-five-year-older version of herself - her mother, red hair and all. She smiled wanly and checked her cell phone often. If it's Saturday, this must be Seattle. If I were her, I'd be praying all of these cameras weren't stealing bits of my daughter's soul. Mom-mager (mom/manager) must rank in the top three most nerve-wracking jobs.

My girls finally ascended the stage. Bella graciously hugged two of them and complimented the third's outfit. "I saw you dancing," she said to them. "I like your style. You guys are cute." Recognition. Acceptance. What we came here for. They levitated away, each clutching a scrap of stardust in the form of an 8x10 glossy of Bella.

On the way home, they were curiously quiet. I peeked at them in the rear-view mirror. They were tweeting away on their cell phones. My daughter caught my eye. "It was awesome, mom. Next time, on that stage - it'll be you!" *Awwwwwww.*

Pussy to the Wood
by Deborah

Some of the best advice on how to be a musician I got from a kid, a street performer named Coy. Coy was singing a song called "Sunshine" by a rap band named Atmosphere (a hip hop band out of Minnesota with rappers named Slug and Ant). This young man on his acoustic guitar, with his simple chord progressions, stopped me in my tracks. I was late to meet friends, but stood riveted, wanting to hear another song. I told this boy I was learning guitar and he said "Two hours. Practice two hours a day."

Really? Two hours. I have to admit I have been practicing barely two minutes. And it is showing, it seems I am the weak link. I have emerged as not only a lead singer, but also the lead guitarist. Let me explain - like some kind of protective inbred royal family, we three girls do not want to add another member to our band. We love each other and have so much fun together, we can't imagine integrating someone else, plus coordinating three schedules is nearly impossible, forget a fourth. So it is clear we all need to multi-task, big time. Rain is the only one who has been seriously taking lessons for some months and it shows, she's back there doing her thing while Kristin and I thrash around, Skyler running back and forth between us.

Two hours isn't possible, but twenty minutes is and I am seeing if this Violet is going to blossom, I need to commit to at least that.

Kristin texted me saying she needed a coach, here was my advice: "Get your sassy self to the keyboard twice per week, even if it is only for five minutes."

That was a reasonable start for her. I have been doing that for a few weeks and am now getting to my guitar more often. It took me a while to find my sweet spot. Right now, I like to practice at night. I grab my acoustic and splay my music all over the bed, sometimes have on a YouTube video to play along with. It's perfect for me, because I am too tired to write in the evenings but want to do something creative. I find, even if I only commit to five minutes, fifteen, sometimes even fifty minutes later, I am still at it.

Some further advice on tenacity, I got from reading about Joan Jett, who is regarded as the "Godmother of Punk" and the "Original Riot Grrrl." Joan had a rock idol named Suzi Quatro, the first female bass guitar player to become a major rock star. Joan copied Suzi's shag haircut and style, waiting long hours just to catch a glimpse of her (she even had Suzi's name carved into her platform shoes). When Joan's solo album was released in 1980, twenty-three record studios rejected it. She and her music partner Kenny Laguna, used Laguna's daughter's college money to start Blackheart Records.

In addition to tenacity, Joan Jett had something else in common with young Coy, the street artist I mentioned above - both created a fresh and original cover. The song that Joan is most famous for, "I Love Rock 'n' Roll," wasn't written by her, but by a band called the Arrows. After many hits and accolades, Joan continued to evolve, Blackheart records produced Bikini Kill, and several other punk and girl bands, and I am sure most satisfying for Joan, punk girl bands.

Joan Jett was unapologetically sexy and rowdy early on in a scene completely devoid of women. The movie *The Runaways* is a raw look at this powerful female's history. The advice Joan gave the actress Kristin Stewart who played her was: "Pussy to the wood!" Great advice for music and so much more!

Dressing the Part
by Kristin

I have kept the first three outfits I wore during our maiden band practices. I finger them when this KaryzMa! needs some extra charisma. Being in a band and living in Olympia offer unique style opportunities, perfect for a girl like me. On the streets of downtown, it is a fashion show everyday - eclectic, home-grown, with more than a dash of grunge! Instead of designer handbags bought at full price, many of us are into thrift store finds, preferring vegan shoes and botanically based makeup.

I fit right in and encourage my boys to find their own style, especially my seven-year-old, Coletrane. He wears a fedora and crafts recycled fabrics at school to make warrior gloves and funky eyewear. I use Violet as a tool to express how I feel, usually wearing an outfit that whispers, but sometimes screams, "Hey world, ask me what I am up to!" Clothing, for me, isn't about the hippest trends. If worn with intention, clothes give others permission to be free and expressive. There are days when only a leotard with a bedazzled spider web will do.

I tend to gravitate toward earthen hues, wanting to feel a friend to nature, but in Olympia, there is endless gray, some days I need to rise above. I beat depression by applying plum to my eyes and pulling on turquoise leg warmers. In addition to needing a lift to combat the weather, I often feel ordinary as a mostly-stay-at-home mama. I look to my Violet ensembles to help bolster my spirits.

In the beginning, I would go to thrift stores the day of band practice and see what outfit called to me. My intention to boost morale found me choosing outlandish glittery, summertime dresses. One in particular comes to mind, straight from a 1930's Cotton Club joint, a very short dress that shimmered in three layers of magenta, gold and hot orange.

It is lovely to have fashion between us Violets, from utilitarian cargos to rainbow knits to ball gowns. I recently arrived at band practice in my penguin pajama pants and my fave soft plaid shirt, nothing frilly. I got to Deborah's house only to discover that she was also in her cozy wozy clothes - well-worn organic cotton shirt and yoga pants. Rain's merlot sweater evoked a desire to ditch the instruments, cuddle up on Deborah's big bed and have a tell all. We did just that.

Next week I will most likely tire of the comfy closet and don my latest find - a cocktail dress with a pair of blush-colored boy shorts and flowery fishnets. Clothing aside, the truth is my birthday suit is my favorite outfit of all, because joy is naked, transparent.

Finding My Singing Muse
by Deborah

Last night, I found my muse in an unassuming soul/rock singer in a tacky downstairs bar in Olympia. Sarah T., the love child of Natalie Merchant and Janis Joplin, took the stage for a benefit. Rain and I couldn't look away. Her band, boldly called the Spread Eagles, is the house band for the Eagles Club. The event was a benefit for Rhythm Fire, hosted by Skyler to raise money to finish a CD featuring all fifteen of RF's kid bands.

Despite noble intentions, the event was not the blockbuster RF had hoped for. A few of us die-hard fans showed up, some donations were pledged by email and phone. I recognized one father from my daughter's recent middle school conferences, turns out he is the principal as well as the math teacher - we were in sparse, but good company. Rain and I, ever students of life, took notes about timing (it was a Sunday night near the end of the school year). I love that Skyler did not bat an eye regarding the half-full house, I would have been tripping over myself with apologies. He braved ahead, even put in a plug for the Eagles, "For only $40 a year plus a $15 joining fee, anyone can become a member, the benefits being a safe, cheap bar and access to hosting events at the lounge and ballroom." Later he told us there was an initiation something or other, I don't think he used the word ceremony, but quipped, "Of which I am sworn to secrecy" to which we retorted, "And are you wearing special underwear?"

Rain and I arrived at seven and thoroughly enjoyed the first two sets: a solo act by a local musician named John Leonard, who was followed by a comedian/story teller, whose main yarn was how she, a punk rocker, became homecoming queen. When it was time for the Spread Eagles, it seemed most of the audience's viable grown-ups headed toward the stage. The five-piece band did all covers: "Black Magic Woman," "Brick House" and "I Will Survive" among them, opening with "Red House," an old blues staple made famous by Jimmy Hendrix, who infused new life into the classic with a five minute guitar riff intro (oh wait, he did that on all of his songs).

Sarah, with her curly locks, voluptuous figure and even more curvaceous voice, had us on the edge of our seats from the get go. We loved several things about her: first of all, that her top slid off her shoulder halfway through the first set and she never righted it; second, she made no eye contact with the audience and if she did open her eyes it was to nod toward her band members or look up at the ceiling; third, she felt the music in her bod; and fourth, her voice was Powerful. She did none of the things I thought you "had" to do to capture an audience. She didn't over-sing, didn't pace back and forth, didn't take the microphone out of the stand.

We talked to Sarah between sets and told her how awesome she was. She shared her musical journey - she had done karaoke for three years, singing only one song. On one of these fateful outings, a musician friend witnessed this one song. He told her about his band and asked if she would be interested in checking them out. She was, and sang the same "Red House" she wowed us with, and the rest is history (in her words, "The drummer put down his drumsticks, said 'I need a smoke,' walked outside and that was that"). She said they had great chemistry from the start. We loved that Goddess Sarah was supported by four hunky guys - two guitarists and two drummers who were willing to be in a band called the Spread Eagles. She mentioned that she needed to open her eyes and we begged her not to.

Finally, she shared that none of them made any money being the house band for the Eagles, rather focused on benefit shows. Again that interesting Eagles plug, again from a very non-conformist type of person, perhaps it is a cult. Regardless, we resonated with the "do it because you love it" and charity angle. She said that once a month they host a dance party, usually with a theme like Hawaiian Luau (yes, they roast a pig) and Prom Night (yes, they have a disco ball). Rain and I almost pulled out our checkbooks, ready to write that $40 check, as we haven't danced at our local dive, the gay bar, for over a year and we do miss getting our groove on. In fact, we got up and gave it a whirl with the Spread Eagles, even though no one else was dancing. We were soon joined by others, most notably a young lad, about twelve, who had killer boxing moves.

Sarah blessed me with her style at just the right moment. I had recently scanned YouTube for hours looking for a female singer I would like to emulate - beginning with Janis Joplin's "Take a Piece of My Heart." I found Janis herself untouchable, but anyone doing her covers, like Faith Hill or Mary J. Bilge, too demure. Sarah was perfect and following her lead, I no longer need to worry about looking anywhere (not even at the audience), but concentrate on the music, touching my soul as I sing.

A Shelf of One's Own
by Rain

Yesterday, I gave myself a shelf. My writings have literally been in the closet - on the floor of my bedroom closet, to be precise. Out of sight, out of mind. Meanwhile, the dining room shelves are filled with board games (or as my daughter calls them, *bored* games), books, photo albums, craft supplies, and a shelf for each of my daughters. I decided I deserved one, too. Funny how little things, like space and resource allotment, speak volumes about self-esteem.

I descended upon the area, consolidating, tossing out. The words *a room of one's own* kept buzzing in my ears. It's the title of an article written in 1929 by seminal feminist author Virginia Woolf. "*A woman must have money and a room of her own if she is to write.*" In the essay, Woolf shows us the danger of not shaping one's own creativity by inventing a sister for Shakespeare, named Judith, who was "as adventurous, as imaginative, as agog to see the world as he was. But she was not sent to school." Judith is forced into marriage by her father and later, pregnant by an actor, dies by her own hand.

Money and a room of her own. The money part, I am cobbling together with nannying jobs and a slash-and-burn approach to my budget. Nannying lets me be the mother I need to be for my children-of-divorce: close at hand and available for rides to play dates, driving school, and ballet classes. I never want the quality of their lives to suffer because their parents' marriage didn't work out. Nannying also keeps me close to The Shelf:

several times a day I can glance over, see that violet shimmer and remember who I am becoming, if I allow myself.

On The Shelf I have placed my favorite memoirs, including Deborah's *The Mother Ship* and one about Virginia Woolf's circle, *Love in Bloomsbury* by Frances Partridge. Also *Changing* by Liv Ullmann, the most feminine memoir I've ever read, and Marlene De Blasi's scrumptious *A Thousand Days in Venice*, recounting her bold decision to marry an Italian man she barely knew and move across the world with him. There are also Kurt Cobain's and Courtney Love's his-and-her journals, and Pattie Boyd's tell-all about her time with George Harrison and Eric Clapton.

A milk crate holds files of ideas, essays and scripts I've written. Amethysts are sprinkled around, and a purple kaleidoscope is propped in their center. "We all are given a kaleidoscope when we are born," a wise friend once told me. "But most people rarely turn theirs to new experiences."

I am turning mine now, with a tingle of wonder and trepidation in the pit of my stomach, to Artist. Here goes! I'm coming out of the closet.

Bushwhacking
by Deborah

Rain described it perfectly when I was complaining about the painful process of learning to play guitar. "Bushwhacking," she said. Yes! That is why I love Rain so much. She says exactly THAT thing I need to hear to make my challenges, my issues, my life make sense. With that one word she transformed my struggle with learning to play guitar into a possible endeavor. Instead of feeling overwhelmed with psychic kudzu, I envisioned myself with a machete cutting new neural pathways. I could see that the next pass would be easier, until a clear trail is laid.

Mark, my vocal teacher, has lately become my guitar teacher as well. Mark is ridiculously talented and will brush off any compliments about guitar playing as he is a singer first, then trumpet player and drummer, guitarist last. But almost any song I suggest, most lately, "Second Hand News" by Fleetwood Mac, he plays and sings on the first go-round, like a Lindsey Buckingham double.

I have a default strum, any new song, any new circumstance (like someone coming over to listen or sing) and I go right to this certain pattern. Up down, down up, down down. Mark and I have been working to break me of it. For two weeks, we had been tackling "Trouble" by Ray La-Montagne and "Angel From Montgomery" by John Prine, performed most notably by Bonnie Raitt. At one point, I could feel my hands wanting to do the old thing instead of the new pattern we had just practiced for the last half hour, but I slowed way down and strummed the new way. I could physically feel the switch in my brain. I thought of what Rain said, laid down my machete (my guitar) and fist-bumped Mark. Yes, my brain may be a deep, tangled jungle, but for the first time, I could see the clearing.

I haven't had much practice re-wiring my body to do my bidding. After about the age of seven, a banner year when I mastered bike riding, rollerskating and swimming, I have been pretty cerebral. Learning to drive a car, skiing and rocking a baby might be the only times I have laid new track, and those were decades ago.

According to neuroscience, making music is the number one human activity that uses more parts of the brain simultaneously than any other. Guitar playing has emboldened me to try other things, among them, snowboarding. I encouraged myself after falling over and over again on the snow, using my confidence on the strings, even as limited as it is. I am wielding my saber, even on the mundane - putting keys in the same place in my purse, every time? Done.

Nibbles from Scout Niblett
by Deborah

In one of those serendipitous moments, Rain and I happened to look up Scout Niblett's website, when we were cyber-searching bands. We had jumped from Counting Crows to the Black Keys to Lady Antebellum to Bjork looking for examples of fine lyrical singers and I thought of Scout's unique style. Scout Niblett's song "Kiss" is my gold standard, I had it on my car stereo for months and I wanted to remind Rain of its genius. We'd never seen Scout's quirky website and clicking on her touring schedule, we saw she was going to be in our little locale within a few weeks.

We had originally discovered Scout in a music video, back at the beginning of the beginning when Kristin and Rain were occasionally hanging out with Palu, the guitarist who had been in our fledging band before we, by default, became an all-girl band. Palu had a studio apartment in a historic building downtown, with enough room for his bicycle, a hot plate and a projector, on which he and the girls would watch obscure movies and YouTube videos. The one night I joined them, I was introduced to Scout's "Kiss," which featured a pretty girl with short pixie hair and a man dressed in a skeleton costume, traipsing amongst autumn leaves harmonizing at the soul level about love, accompanied by a haunting guitar. I downloaded "Kiss" on my iPod and played it continually, do to this day. It is the one song that I most love to sing along with.

The show was at the Backstage Theatre at the Capitol - it is literally that, an area as big as a large living room, behind a movie screen. The performers on stage face the "wrong way." The tickets were cheap, eight dollars. I think we were the only ones who actually bothered to buy pre-sold tickets and not pay at the door. The cashier at Rainy Day Records, an Olympia staple, had assured me, "Scout Niblett? That won't sell out. Guaranteed." Geez, have some respect, I thought. We bought tickets anyway.

Ever the fashionistas, Rain and I were both horrified and humbled by Scout's concert attire. She wore red knee socks (like the soccer socks my boys wear over shin guards), cut off jean shorts and a baggy rumpled navy sweater which was long in the sleeves and high in the neck. Not an inch of skin distracted us from her performance. Her hair was pulled back in a messy ponytail and she wore no makeup. I wondered if Scout had planned this, just-running-to-the-store-for-some-Pepto-Bismol look on purpose to make a statement or if she was just clueless. I expected her to look classier, given her video and the picture of her in the paper, which showed her with a styled pageboy haircut and wearing a sheath-y vintage dress. Another option is that she was about as inspired to play in Olympia as Olympia was un-inspired to host her, we may have not seemed worth the dry cleaning.

No matter, we loved all of it. Loved that she didn't seem to give a hoot, that the other two members of her band, two guys in button-down shirts and jeans that actually fit, were more stylish than her. Loved learning later that she (Emma Louise Niblett) had pen named herself Scout from the classic book, *To*

Kill A Mockingbird, and we loved googling her images to see how she shape-shifts.

Speaking of the other two guys. The drummer was dishy, tall and dark-haired, the bass player, an aged rocker type complete with goatee. What I noticed most about them, was that they were in complete service to dear Scout. They watched her every move and adjusted, like one organism. The drummer especially was finest attuned, and if they aren't a couple, I would be surprised.

Like Sarah T. (the other female vocalist we had recently seen from the local band, the Spread Eagles), Scout did not talk to us or look at us, with one exception to ask towards the end, "Is there anything else? Any requests?" To which I pitched again, "Kiss?!" as I had been interjecting between every song transition. She granted my wish and I melted as it sounded just as amazing as the recording. I couldn't help but join quietly in (ok, not so quietly), despite the girl in front of us who kept turning and looking at me. Couldn't tell if her smile was a genuine impressed-ness or annoyance, but I was not going to stop (two drinks in, after all). I had dozens of hours honing my harmonies on this one.

Scout's other moment of note was a soulful rendition of Paul McCartney's "Maybe I'm Amazed." Love it when a girl sings a guy's song well. Although, unfortunately it didn't end there. For her last turn, she went to the drums and played a solo like an amateur but with attitude, singing a tongue-in-cheek medley of "We Are the World," which she alternated with her own verse, "We are all going to die." Hmmm... True. I just would rather not be reminded of that.

Then, anticlimactically, she said, "Well, I guess that's it," and scurried off to the merchandise table where she looked much smaller than she had on stage. We joined her, with praise aplenty, to which she apologized for the poor sound quality and seemed quite distraught the concert had not gone better. None of the compliments Rain or I lavishly offered could assuage her.

We left feeling defeated, noting to ourselves, at the end of a concert, no matter how it went, be in the present moment, meet your fans with a smile, *hear* and *receive* the love they are bestowing upon you. Yes, we heard the amp tweak a few times. We were too distracted to care and actually found it refreshing - shit happens. We were focused on Scout's voice, her guitar playing, the gestalt of the band and her awesomeness. None of which she seemed to be able to take in. And in her self-berating state, she did not acknowledge us, her enthusiastic fans, at all. It is a gift to say, "I am thankful that I touched you and please honor yourself, that you may be moved."

If I Lay Here
by Deborah

Recently, I was on hold waiting for a supervisor with the United States Citizenship Immigration Service, trying to get some information regarding the Permanent Resident Green cards that never showed up over a year ago for my adopted boys. What I didn't know is whether the cards had been sent and lost or never sent; irregardless, I was told I needed to spend another four hundred dollars (each) to replace them and take my boys to Seattle for biometrics (sounds worse than it is - height, weight and fingerprints, but still a supreme hassle). I had been going round and round with this for weeks, into the social security office three times trying to prove the boys really were adopted so I could get social security numbers to file taxes, hoping to get eight hundred dollars back from Uncle Sam, not give that much more.

"May I put you on hold?" the overwhelmed employee asked and I began to cry. In the next moment, some bars of piano came over the phone system of the office of Homeland Security... it was a simple melody, a bit garbled even. But not too garbled that I couldn't hear lyrics about lying with a lover, forgetting the world.

I pressed my cell phone as close to my ear as I could, hearing the opening bars, then the first verse and chorus. I knew suddenly why I had to go through this ordeal, why the residence cards were lost, why I adopted those boys, why I was even born. Here my feelings are echoed in a post by BrinkOblivion, on YouTube:

This song makes me wanna strip naked, burst out of my window, free fall twenty-eight floors, face plant in the snow, make a snow angel mixed with my own blood, shiver from the cold, get hypothermia, DIE, go the pearly gate, say wuzzup to Jesus, do our secret hand shake, look for Buddha, find him, have him reincarnate me into a frog, meet a princess, kiss her, turn into a prince, order my subjects to bring me a computer, listen to this song again, cry myself to sleep. Wake up... Repeat.

The band is Snow Patrol, from Northern Ireland, the song is called "Chasing Cars." The song is a simple chord progression, A-D-E, same three chords in most Bob Dylan songs, the chords I am using in the upbeat "Second Hand News" by Fleetwood Mac, and "Angel From Montgomery" by John Prine. The lead singer is named, appropriately, Gary Lightbody. "If I Lay Here" explained the longing I have to just be myself and be loved, to have my crazy world pause while I luxuriate in someone's arms, to finally be home. Months later, I sang this song to my boyfriend and cried while he held me, experiencing what often only music can give - a medium to express our deepest yearnings.

Moving Away From Violet
by Kristin

Last summer my husband Michael and I decided to move full-time to a tiny resort town called Union, forty-five minutes away from Olympia. Michael is the executive chef at a sweet restaurant on the Hood Canal called the Robin Hood. He had been living part-time in Union and the commute was killing me, as he currently has no driver's license, which makes me the designated driver. I was done driving all over creation and curious to see if a small town would suit me better. Our marriage was improving, after a few separations over the past three years, and we knew that we needed to be together as a family.

To be honest, I wanted time away from Violet. I was tired of feeling like I wasn't pulling my weight. I stopped practicing with them a few months before I moved to Union, blamed it on feeling fragmented: playing chauffeur to the children and Michael, being responsible for the kids' well-being, keeping up with the housework, all the while battling my ongoing feelings of depression. I did not feel resonant with the keyboard, and wasn't sure of my role with Violet if I didn't play an instrument. I told Rain and Deborah that I still wanted to participate by coming to meetings once a month, but I was not sure if even that would happen. I hoped if I was not distracted and could get a grip on my moods, I might be able to integrate myself fully back into the band.

My family and I left Olympia, excited and nervous to see what it would be like to live in a town that doesn't even have a stoplight. A friend once called Union "a place where the heart and soul unite." I have always wanted to live in an A-frame and we manifested one immediately. My hubby prefers to live in the forest, and sure enough, our little home backed right up to tall evergreens and glorious maples. We were surrounded by bird call and even had a little brown bear visit our backyard for a few weeks. Gazing out a sliding glass door one morning, I made eye contact with a red fox passing through our quiet cul-de-sac. Our house came furnished, and Michael and I found ourselves enveloped in a king-sized bed for the first time. We even had our own private bathroom that looked out over a well-manicured golf course. There were times when I could read the energy of the golfer. I stood tall like the trees that surrounded the course and tried to absorb the concentration that a golfer must possess.

I got a job at a renowned cancer retreat center, Harmony Hill, just down the way from my home. I have always been attracted to eradicating cancer because my best friend in high school fought the disease back in our early thirties. Ultimately her physical body was not up to speed with her spirit and she passed on at a very early age in life. She is a guardian angel to me now and I feel her smile every day. The founder of Harmony Hill, Gretchen Schodde, is now my mentor in all things. She had a vision that kept her up at night - to create a philanthropic community which gives free retreats to people with cancer. I am proud to be part of such a soulful, grateful group of people. I started in housekeeping, which segued into a hospitality position.

Gretchen offered me more than a job, she has given me a calling. She has taken me under her wing and is a great resource to me in terms of attracting investors for my husband's dream, a restaurant/communal artisan space. Working on my relationship with money is of the utmost importance. I am helping Gretchen arrange her home and office, an essential component of feeling balanced. I am extrapolating my lesson, visualizing Violet creating abundance.

Last but not least, I have my best friend Suzi Struger in Union. Suzi doles out Laws of Attraction (the belief that we create our own reality with our thoughts) tidbits to one and all. She has survived cancer, but more important than that, she lives and breathes abundance, using words like *vortex, allowing, Source and contrast.* Suzi keeps her vibration radically clean; she does not tell me stories about the strife in her life, because that would be bringing up the vibration all over again. Instead, she blesses the hard people and situations she has attracted because they help her realize what she truly wants. When I arrive in despair about a relationship, she coos, "Honey, rather than tell me the details of the fight, can you see how crystal clear it is that you want relationships in your life that are supportive and affirming?" I am not there yet, but my gossiping has fallen by the wayside and I feel myself tasting the peace she radiates.

I quickly integrated into Union, with Harmony Hill and folks like Suzi feeding my spirit. My other haunts are the old world pub at the Robin Hood Restaurant and the only cafe in Union (where my girlfriends, who are my lifeline, work). At times my idyllic house in the woods can feel very masculine-oriented, with the boys and my Michael. I simply pack a bag, head to the cafe for a cup o' joe and catch up with my goddess friends. I then zoom over to the marina, park at the boat launch, and enjoy my last sips of coffee while I walk up and down the little pebble beach and talk to my bald eagle friends, juveniles mostly. In the winter not even the gray skies and pelting cold rain bug me, the Hood Canal holds me in a state of unrefined bliss.

After my prayers are scattered on the beach and my intentions litter the landscape, I head back to the car to settle in. Writing pad and pen in hand, my thoughts turn to affirmations on paper and as I breathe and chant, "Om Shanti," creative musings stir. The last time I was there, I sang and wrote, "I am an integral part of this vast Universe, my connection is palpable. I can be a part of Violet, I can be gentle with myself, I am worthy and achieve wholeness through balance. Grace is possible."

Where Two or More Are Gathered
by Deborah

Kristin has decided to pull back from the band for a while, perhaps forever. There has been much gnashing of teeth over this, mostly on her end as she has felt torn in too many directions. Physically, she has moved out of Olympia to Union. Psychically, she is tapped as well, mothering her little ones, the youngest of the Violet tribe, only three and six years old.

Both Rain and I remember when ours were smaller, how hard it was to commit to anything, seemed someone was always sick or up the previous night. Rain and I both had our kids in Waldorf schools at one point. At a parent meeting, I learned the founder, Rudolf Steiner's philosophy that children are in your aura, in your "bubble" basically, drawing on your energy, until they are seven. I have felt this with each of my own kids and my youngest son just turned eight. For Kristin, this merging was textbook illustrated by her six-year-old, who was crushed when she discussed leaving Violet out loud, "You cannot quit!" he told her emphatically. Quit is a strong verb and none of us are as dramatic as any of that, to quit the band sounds so high school.

On the downside, Rain and I had been counting on Kristin's charisma and potential keyboarding skills to round us out. Egads, we were now officially a duo. That's not really a band is it? Plus Kristin was the token brunette.

It took two or three happy hours, but Rain and I felt more in than ever. We didn't for a moment consider abandoning our dream. In our favor, we two seemed to be the main driving force anyway; we regularly meet up to talk about Violet, practice a little, and talk about Violet some more. We soothed ourselves by looking to bands like the White Stripes for inspiration. Yes, the drummer is ridiculously talented and the lead singer is a genius, but so what. Recently we had seen a band called Hillstomp which is two guys, two instruments, always a toe-tapping crowd.

I have been using the phrase, *where two or more are gathered* to boost Rain and I. Like many, I use it to describe the synergy that happens when more than one person endeavors to do something (totally morphing the meaning from the biblical interpretation which has to do more with identifying sinners). We take inspiration that there are usually two names you remember in any band: Mick Jagger and Keith Richards of the Rolling Stones, Paul McCartney and John Lennon of the Beatles, Sting and Stewart Copeland of the Police. We figured we needed to jack up our ass power and, oh yeah - practice a lot more.

I Still Want to Hold Your Hand
by Rain

We have been learning The Beatles' "I Want to Hold Your Hand" for six months now. That's a whole lot of *I can't hide*'s... We meet three times a month, for an hour, with Skyler, who looks like Paul McCartney with a smidge of garden gnome. Deborah and I sit down at our instruments, give each other a little ironic tilt of the eyebrow, and have yet another go at it. During the week, we get together once or twice to assimilate the latest refinements that Skyler has given us.

In our defense, it's not the simplest of songs. The guitar chords are many and varied. We are doing the slow, sultry version that was featured on the *Across the Universe* movie soundtrack. It is stripped down, with little more than acoustic guitar. Skyler is encouraging me to figure out my own drumming. This has led us into many unexpected learning moments. "You're swinging that second snare hit," Skyler will note. *I'm what??!* "You're delaying it. That's a swing beat, not a rock beat." *Is that wrong?* It is if you're doing the song with a rock beat, apparently. Swing is more jazzy. You can hear it on Blind Melon's "No Rain." Ti-*diih*-dih-ti-*diih*-dih... I really like swing beat and keep dropping into it. But a good drummer needs to do both. Blindfolded.

One major area of growth has been weaning ourselves from the original track. Early on, we needed to play along with it a few times before venturing off on our own. Now we get right down to playing our version. Even though we are still in utero as musicians, we at least have the rudiments of a skeletal system to start from.

We have begun working on the Pretenders' "Back on the Chain Gang" as well to preserve our sanity. We decided to slow this song down, too, to really let the lyrics stand out. Deborah jokes that we will be to bands what large print is to books. But our own style is FINALLY emerging: when I can steady myself enough to drop down deep into the groove, and Deborah's fingers discipline themselves at the fret bar, her voice holds something magic. There's a woodland creature in her soul and it's exhilarating when it comes out to play. We imagine ourselves, in the misty future, tucked into a corner of a cafe or a wine bar, weaving a delicate web of intimacy and intricacy. Yes, holding hands with the audience... hopefully ours won't be sticky and sweaty.

Can You Feel My Disease?
by Deborah

I was recently at a hole in the wall in Olympia, a bar connected to a barbecue joint, called the Pig. The bar is about the size of a family room den, painted red, complete with comfy leather couches. I was amazed I hadn't been there before. Amazed at all the grown-ups, seems I have been frequenting places where only twenty-one-year-olds hang out. Nice to see some gray hair and crow's feet. I felt positively young.

And welcomed - before I'd even had a sip of my beer, I met a couple who handed me a business card inviting me to their annual Badminton doubles tournament next July. All the pertinent details were printed: The party lasts from ten a.m. to ten p.m. (although they said they went until four a.m. last year) and you needed to wear whites. An italicized quote read, *Shuttlecock. If you can say it, you can play it.* This has provided me with countless chuckles.

I followed my friends for their smoke break and as they inhaled away, I stepped outside the secondhand haze and noticed a little trollish man walking by. He was hunchbacked almost, looking down at the sidewalk. I felt a surge of pity and assumed, "Oh, that guy must have a sad life."

Ten minutes later, back in the Pig, the band had begun and Mr. Hunch stepped up to the keyboard. I was blown away. More blown away when he started singing "Come Together" by the Beatles with virility that would put any GQ magazine model to shame. The choice of music was ironic (walrus gumboot and all), but my new inspiration owned it, with a presence I have yet to muster.

My lesson, as I watched this "toe-jam-football" man sing and bang on the keyboard with a zeal that was positively sexy? As I ponder if I am too old, too ugly, too wide to play music? To do anything? Appearances don't matter. Anyone, anyone can be anybody. Anyone who is willing to feel and express their soul. Passion and its outward gift, charisma, are available to us all. The only disease that night? My own judgement.

Cover Me
by Deborah

Most often the songs I choose to cover are ones I hear on the radio, even though that is pretty paleolithic in these iTunes times. I will however, include Pandora in the mix, my teenagers have finally hooked me up. Restaurants and coffee shops are also great places to be exposed to music, I often chose them based on their playlists. Applebee's, despite being part of a chain, has a great soundtrack. Rain and I like to joke that after two drinks, everything is a cover. I am embarrassed to admit how many times I have been buzzed and written down the songs, "Sweet Home Alabama" and "Freebird." "Blackbird" by the Beatles is also a topper.

Sometimes original artists move me enough to attempt to emulate them and sometimes it is hearing a second artist's re-interpretation and I end up covering a cover. I was once at a bar (egads, again!) and k.d. lang came on, singing "Helpless" by Neil Young. A woman two stools over harmonized in a nice alto and by the time the song was halfway done, there were bets as to the song, the original artist and the meaning. This wonderful classic, freshly done, had the whole bar stop our individual banter and unite. Bonnie Raitt did the same for John Prine's "Angel from Montgomery." "Sweet Child O' Mine" is another tune I enjoy, the original is by Guns 'n' Roses, but it was Sheryl Crow who inspired me to give it a whirl.

I can tell the twists and turns in my life by the covers I am drawn to, from "What Kind of Fool" by Barbra Streisand and

Barry Gibb, to my current fave, "One Step Up" by Bruce Springsteen. The latter perfectly describes the feeling I had in my love relationship at its lowest point. My guy and I kept having the same issues and I felt we were growing farther apart. Springsteen's lyrics capture this poignantly.

A few months of singing about "two steps back" (combined with therapy!) resulted in me moving through my fear, sadness and anger. My man and I navigated this difficult time, and yet still, I sing this song. It reminds me to stay awake, to not let an hour, let alone days, go by without clear communication. Around this time, while I was getting gas, "Into the Mystic" by Van Morrison was playing at the pumps and I was drawn to its mood of freedom and celebration.

The following is my flow chart for choosing covers:

1. Does the song move me? Do I whip out my phone and take notes or try to find out what it is?
2. Do I have the skills now, can I play it?
3. After I have played it a few times, am I still interested?

"One Step Up" fascinates me, as a singer, as a fledgling guitar player a year in, even after my love life improved. "Into the Mystic" moved in and out rapidly, there were places it tripped me. "Sweet Child" is another song I have kept in my back pocket. Although written about a lover, I like to think about my thirteen-year-old daughter when I sing it.

I have learned to let songs go, likening them to relationships; we fall in love all the time, with lovers, friends, mentors, ideas - only time reveals who we choose to make our own. Some songs, like some people and places, journey with us forever.

The Drums Have Left the Building
by Rain

A Man has moved into my room. For a while, he inched around my burgundy and chrome drum kit on his trek between bed and bathroom, his own belongings piled in a corner. He is an organized man, a simple man, and a man with his own plan for world domination through writing. He needed a desk. He needed a *place*.

The feng shui experts say if you want to manifest a bed partner, make sure your room invites one. After five years of separation and divorce, I was ready to extend that invitation; to whom, I knew not yet. But when I saw the paint-splattered Ikea side table in the "free" bin at my friend's apartment building, I scooped it up and placed it on the opposite side of my queen-sized bed. And waited.

Not even a week later, the man of my dreams unexpectedly showed up. He was disguised in a grumpy Beast costume, but I could tell there was a prince lurking in there somewhere. Our relationship evolved and he asked to move in. I said yes, to air tinged with faint traces of transmission fluid, black dog, and secondhand books, yes, to an intense love I had yet to experience. To quote Christopher Marlowe:

come live with me and be my love, and we will all the pleasures prove...

All the pleasures, that is, except having a rousing drum roll pelting into your right eardrum. Did I mention he is a simple man, a quiet man? A man who got really excited when he discovered my medieval a cappella CD by the Anonymous Four (a cappella: *singing without instrumental accompaniment*). I'll be the first to admit that the drums fall into that category of musical instruments that are far more fun to play than to listen to *being* played. Beginning violin also comes to mind, as does the tuba. I looked long and hard at those shiny skins, filling up half of the room. They looked good. The Man looked even better.

A ceremonial relocation was in order. One by one, we picked up each drum and carried it reverently to its new home - the garage. We set them up under a window, and stepped back to gauge the effect. I was secretly afraid that I would practice less, without them staring me in the face from my bed. "I know these are your babies," The Man said. "You must really love me."

It turns out I didn't practice any less. Most of my drumming practice takes place in the car, anyway, where I can turn the stereo up loud. Something about the confined space and the forward motion seems to focus my attention on music, rather than, say, on the road. Stopped at a red light, I rifle through my loose CDs and fish out something inspirational. Lately, it's been 90's band the Sundays' three albums (remember "Here's Where the Story Ends"?).

The Sundays are particularly encouraging to me, as the founding couple had no musical background and taught themselves guitar and vocals while collecting unemployment benefits after university. My kind of people! It is perhaps just this DIY approach that lends their music an originality in composition and arrangement that keeps me listening, year after year. My left leg starts pumping to the kick drum, I start counting "one two three four" to see where the taut snap of the snare is landing, my left fingers tap out the hi-hat cymbal, and before you know it, the car behind me is leaning on his horn. Joining in, I like to think.

Speaking of do-it-yourself, I was pleasantly startled to hear the distant boom and crash of my drum kit from the garage when my daughter's friend was visiting. "We've started a band!" they informed me. Just think - how many twelve-year-old girls have unlimited access to a drum kit? Not nearly enough, anyway.

Fire and Ice, First Concert
by Deborah

I recently took two of my older kids to a concert, my daughter, Karina's first. Ed Sheeran, a solo act from Britain, opened for Snow Patrol at the Paramount in Seattle. Karina has relished being one of Sheeran's first fans and when we found out he was coming to the Northwest a few months ago it was a no-think to get tickets. They seemed ridiculously cheap at thirty-one bucks compared to the usual headliners, which are about triple that. So cheap, I splurged and bought myself, her best friend, Kayta, and my sixteen-year-old son, Misha, seats as well. This concert was general admission, although the space was divided in two sections, the Orchestra and Balcony. Unfortunately, the Orchestra seats were sold out and we were only able to get up-top ones, but we decided to go early enough to at least be in the front row.

As we drove into the city at five p.m, we learned Seattle was having a May Day, Occupy Wall Street-style protest. The disenchanted (calling themselves the Black Bloc) had broken windows at several banks and flagship stores and lit a few luxury cars on fire. In response, the city teemed with SWAT vans and helicopters. With everyone's attention a few blocks further downtown, the evening unfolded as if we rode a magic carpet. For two Paramount shows I had attended, parking was remote at best; for this, I glided right into a spot across from the parked tour bus of the band.

There were only a dozen-plus people in line, camped out across from the marquee, and we joined, umbrellas and gloves in hand. Karina had been suggesting all day that she would meet her idol, Sheeran, and although I am usually affirming to the point of annoyance, I had tried to gently dissuade her so she wouldn't be disappointed. Despite my attempts, she went so far as to proclaim, "I am so glad I got to meet Ed Sheeran!"

About an hour after we arrived, Misha went to our minivan to charge his phone and saw a white car delivering Sheeran (who had been tweeting like a blue jay all afternoon, "Not sure how I will get to the gig, with Seattle in riots"). My boy quickly alerted the girls, who left the line and joined a handful of lucky fans. Sheeran was relaxed and friendly; he posed for several pictures with my crew while I dealt with the world's friendliest scalper.

I had approached the seller thinking he could "upgrade" the girls to Orchestra seating, which he could, for forty dollars a ticket. Seemed fair enough; I didn't even think to haggle, partially because he was from Olympia, grew up a few miles away from our home, mostly because I am a wimp at bartering, don't even do it in Mexico. At first I only bought two tickets, then another for my son, relishing that I would still be in the balcony on a chair, resting my first-day-of-period legs. However, my new friend, the "broker," convinced me I should share this experience with my kids and I bought the fourth ticket, almost doubling my initial "bargain" investment.

The Paramount doors opened at seven, an hour before the show was to begin. Even though we were sure we would be in the first row, given how far up we were in line, we ended up in the third, overtaken by seasoned concert goers who blatantly ignored the personnel admonishing, "Don't run!" We were close enough, though, and enjoyed the next hour anticipating the bands in our newly coveted real estate, a few square feet of floor space where we could sit, a perk for my throbbing legs.

We met two super cute twenty-somethings next to us, one reminiscent of a young Cyndi Lauper and the other a younger Joni Mitchell. Cyndi got busy scoping out the merch table and making song request signs for Sheeran while Joni promised us Snow Patrol would be amazing, this was her fourth time seeing them. The buzz around us was just that. I overheard a woman ticking off groups including U2 and R.E.M., concluding Snow Patrol put on the best show. I was excited to hear "Chasing Cars," but otherwise, knew nothing about the band.

Ed Sheeran played a much too quick half-hour set, performing only four songs, but was so present, so talented we were not disappointed by the brevity; he also promised to be back, headlining in the fall. He demonstrated his use of a loop recorder where he lays down tracks of vocals, percussion and guitar licks, which repeat, layering a band before our eyes. Karina was thrilled. Ed has some clever branding; having red hair (as does my daughter), he enhances that uniqueness by wearing orange. My girl got herself an orange rubber bracelet embossed with his name and his other brand, a paw print.

Snow Patrol didn't make us wait long to prove the reputation that had preceded them. Gary Lightbody came out like a comet, his thin, tall body filling the stage, arms in the air, legs spread wide, smile even wider. I glanced at Misha, who had the same thought, "Wow, this guy loves performing." Gary then shocked us all, halfway into the first song, he ran toward the audience, tripped and fell, ending up on his back at the lip of the stage. He was a mere ten feet from us, prone on the ground. He paused a moment, as shocked as the crowd, righted himself and proclaimed, "That is what happens sometimes, we fall down and we get back up!"

Masterful.

Lightbody continued to wow us for almost two hours, carrying the entire band on his megawatt charisma. Although not classically handsome, he is a stunner - think a lanky Hugh Grant without the cheekbones and with more hair. The other bandmates (and there were lots of them, three drummers in all) ranged from looking interested to indifferent, to finally, wasted (the lead guitarist looked like Edward from the movie, *Twilight,* and like he'd had as much sleep). Lightbody was enough though, especially when Sheeran joined him for an a cappella version of Snow Patrol's heartfelt song, "New York."

What Made the Concert Wonderful:

1. cool graphics of animated birds, eagles and owls flying over different landscapes as a backdrop
2. the positive message of many of Snow Patrol's songs
3. the way the crowd loved and knew their music, the diversity of the crowd, twenty-something guys next to forty-something moms

4. the constant appreciation of us, the audience
5. the constant appreciation of life, of friends, of music, of Seattle, of 90's music that influenced them (including Peter Buck from R.E.M. who was among the spectators)
6. the varying tempos of song and mood; they led the audience in a call-and-response, "Hush your mouth and sing to me," first had us whisper and then whipped us to a frenzy
7. the focus of the band was on having a conversation with the crowd, not so much with each other; never had I been so included in a show

On the drive home, my children were abuzz with the evening, everything from seeing Sheeran before the show, to the unexpected talent of Snow Patrol. I was glad I would be included in their memory.

The Moon and Sixpence
by Rain

When I say money is tight this month, I mean that I found myself warning my girls to take it easy on the toilet paper. "Three sheets to a pee!" my older one replied breezily. We went across town to the other branch of the pet supply store (where we wouldn't be recognized as repeat offenders) for free puppy food samples. For the dog, not us! We had sixty whole dollars for our weekly food budget - forty less than usual. Rather a challenge, especially with a sixteen-year-old ballerina/gourmet chef with the metabolism of a racehorse. "We can be like our Irish ancestors," I suggest. "Stay in bed all day to conserve strength." That got me the hairy-eyeball stare.

Then, the phone rang. It was my friend Wendy, wanting to rendezvous at a mall midway between our two towns. The mall! That is just a heartache waiting to happen for us po' folks. It's amazing all the stuff you never knew you needed. But, we DID need to see these friends, to get our shine on. Some people just do that for you, and those are the ones you need to seek out. With a big "Don't ask for anything!" warning from me, we headed out the door, thanking the powers-that-be for our fuel efficient car.

We met up in the clothing store, Forever 21. Chandeliers glittered overhead and the 80's music dared to imply:

Recession? What recession?! Nothing but unending prosperity and baby doll florals in here!

My friend Wendy gave me a massive hug and said, "I'm STARVING! Let's eat!" (What, again? We just ate yesterday!) There was nothing for it but to mosey over to the food court. I nursed a coffee and focused on the conversation. When Wendy was full, my racehorse grazed happily on her leftovers.

Next, to shop, chat, laugh, discover, enjoy. Wendy bought herself a beaded turquoise cuff bracelet, very fetching. My younger daughter spent an hour in the Sephora cosmetics store/heaven. Did you know there was such a thing as spray-on foundation? Neither did I, until I saw the makeup artist blow-drying her client's face after application. I reveled in the luscious mineral colors of the eye shadows and the giddy scents of perfume. Finally, I directed my daughter's attention to the $3 shelf. Really? Really! She carefully selected a lip gloss.

Back to Forever 21, Wendy re-vamped her wardrobe. I got a contact high, fondling silky tops and fawn-colored boots and imagining them on her. "Mori Girl," she informed me. "It's a Japanese fashion that means Girl of the Forest. It's my style." I liked it too, though you'd have to throw in a little Debbie Harry to suit me.

We were nearing the checkout counter, the end of a long but rewarding day, when I spotted it. The Bracelet. Unabashed links of bling that fit together like chain mail, held together by an incongruous turquoise string. I hesitated. I slipped it on. It molded to my wrist as if it had grown there. Nine dollars. Groan. Wendy sidled up to me. "Oh, yes," she purred. My brain did little budget backflips, but my heart was already steering my obedient legs toward the counter.

That day, my older daughter learned she could have as much fun buying one shirt as two, from her babysitting stash. "That way I still have money, if my friends want to go the the movies or something," she reasoned. My younger girl discovered she can sample a whole store worth of cosmetics and walk away with a tiny goody bag to remember it by. And I was reminded that woman does not live by bread alone. The heavy "chink" sound, the glint of my bracelet in the corner of my eye, reminds me how important the promise of unending prosperity, of beauty, is in our lives. And when it shows up, unexpectedly - leap all over it.

Out by the cars, Wendy and I clicked our bracelets together. Shazam! Wonder Women! Now, what can we scrounge up for dinner?

No Crystal, Plenty of Gold
by Deborah

On the way to my music lessons, first playing guitar with Skyler and then singing with Mark, I was feeling a bit anxious, a lot excited. I had decided to really make a go of it and answering to these two sweeties motivates me. Rain and I, as Violet, are still too new to rely on one another, playing music is like jumping in without life preservers, both of us flail around. The anxiety was because it feels edgy to play guitar, edgy to sing loud and with passion, all of what would be asked of me for the next hour plus. I said a prayer on the way in, for magic and ease and a wonderful time, for affirmation that this is the right thing to be doing now.

Skyler and I are working on "Second Hand News" by Fleetwood Mac, with me playing the simple chords A, D and E, while he rips lead on the bass guitar and sings the higher harmony. We know a song is timeless when a thirty-year-old musical genius and a forty-something wannabe fist bump one another after playing together. Mark and I hadn't seen each other for months, and I told him right off I wanted to work on a set list he and I could perform someday, somehow.

Mark and I began our music lesson with our age-old debate - he wants me to sing really loud but doing so, I lose all connection to the song. He argues, "You have to make it dynamic!" I feel I am yelling. I mentioned Norah Jones and Margo Timmins from the Cowboy Junkies and he yawned. A half an hour later, we found a middle ground and were patting ourselves on the back, when he mentioned that his house band was looking for a singer. Seems the lead they have now does really well for the biker crowd venues, but can be a bit over the top (or not have enough top on) for other gigs. They were auditioning a new gal soon, but Mark (the head honcho who makes the band decisions) likes to have a few variations and asked if I would be interested in singing at the ski lodge at Crystal Mountain a few months from now.

I'd like to put in a plug here for the Universe answering one's prayers. Last New Year's Eve, I was at Alpental Ski Lodge with my beau, enjoying a band perform to a roomful of rowdy skiers who were happily bringing in the new year with beer and bluesy rock. I watched the lead singer for a while, then turned to my guy and said, "I could do that and it would be sooo much fun!" An hour later, we took a drive and parked in a quiet cul-de-sac underneath a magical mountain we dubbed "The Matterhorn." Now, less than a year later, my man is living on that very street and I was preparing a set list to sing at a ski resort. Mark caught the wave of this, citing one of his favorites phrases, "Sweet as!"

Turned out Crystal Mountain was more of a strip mine than a sparkling vein. Out of the blue, the management cancelled Mark's contract without explanation. Our next lesson started in a shroud of mourning, images of us rosy-cheeked from the slopes and songs no longer a reality. Sounds dramatic, but it was very disappointing for us both.

Mark and I kept going, and about a month after that I was asked by my friend, Carmen, a teacher of a History of Rock class a local community college, if we would perform a set and be interviewed. A real gig, to real people who cared about music. Of course, we would.

One of the gifts of not being twenty anymore is having a broader scope to my life and seeing that there are natural cycles that play out, things we set in motion must be completed before others can begin. It was a whole year after my boyfriend and I were enjoying the mountains, that a house in the area opened up for him; he wasn't ready before that. The weekend I would have been singing at Crystal was the weekend I rented my first snowboard. If I had spent my energy getting ready for Mark's gig, I might not have taken that plunge this year. Learning to carve turns has given me as much satisfaction as any guitar chord I have attempted.

J. Lo's Nugget of Wisdom
by Kristin

I was recently drawn to an entertainer who has had her share of tabloid fever. Jennifer Lopez (J. Lo), known for booty shaking and co-creating drama, has not been someone I was interested in until a magazine found its way into my lap last week. J. Lo was on the cover in all her glory: heavy makeup, kick-ass blood red dress, pouty lips. Upon seeing her, I immediately thought of the apple the snake gave Eve and I couldn't help but open up to her interview.

In the article, she said that she was insecure about her talent in the past, that she never really gave herself any credit and because of that nobody else did either. J. Lo remarked that we all mirror what the world mirrors to us. Her recent ex-husband, Marc Anthony, told her in the beginning of their relationship that her voice was beautiful, she just had to get out there, it was a "confidence thing."

Reading those words in the article was affirming for me because my dad and his ex-wife used to refer to me as their "little project." They somehow knew that if I could only commit to a goal, success would surely be mine. That was twenty years ago. I have a million interests and have not followed through on any of my ideas of becoming a life coach, an entrepreneur, a school teacher or a barista. When I read the quote about confidence, I burst into tears because that's what it is... a CONFIDENCE thing! I have decided to recommit to Violet, become a writer and a musician. And thank god, I have the maturity to know I don't need the externals like J. Lo's booty to succeed. I only need to stick with it.

Deborah told me yesterday to apply the phrase *slow and steady wins the race* to all things Violet. It all sounds so easy in theory, but in reality, every day I put off writing and practicing... until this week. Building confidence is not something applause can do for you, it is a verb, a practice that requires the loving attention you give to your child.

In the interview, Jennifer explained how lost she once felt. I so appreciated her vulnerability, that she was willing to share her learning process. My mothering has allowed me to instill confidence in my children, now it is my turn.

First Real-ish Gig
by Deborah

A year after Violet played at the Black Lake Grange, two years after Rain offered this daring desire to form a band, I performed in a band-ish kind of way. This first gig was another Rhythm Fire Showcase, another exercise in playing for the choir, but playing nonetheless. Mark and I had been working on a set list for this and for the History of Rock class, which was a few days later. We had three songs: "Sweet Child O' Mine" by Guns 'n' Roses, "Helpless" by Neil Young and revisiting "Can't Let Go" by Lucinda Williams. In the third song, Mark and I were joined by Skyler.

This time, unlike our first outing at the grange, I had really prepared. I had practiced enough, every day as the date approached, memorizing lyrics and chords, all the while, trying to tap into the emotion of the songs, why I was drawn to them in the first place.

A few hours before my "gig," Kristin, acting as my head cheerleader, came over with her two sons. I went through the set in my bedroom, having an audience of several little boys (mine included) helped calm my nerves. I then allowed myself one beer. Mark forewarned about drinking before playing, he has seen the diminishing returns - how getting a little loose can quickly spiral into sloppiness, forgetting lines and transitions. We gussied up and headed to the Eagles club where all the RF gigs are held now, a venue a hundred times better than the grange, as grown-ups can have a drink, there is a pool table and food can be brought in. Plus there is gold foil wallpaper behind the stage which photographs very retro and Violet-y.

Up before us were two bands. The first featured Mark's daughter, Chloe, who at sixteen, has as much presence as Lady Gaga. Mark's twelve-year-old son, Manny, was solid on the drums. A girl named Kelsey (who took piano lessons with my kids) has evolved into another enviable front woman and a few other protégés rounded out the sound. It has been fun to watch Kelsey and Chloe's evolution - they now jump around, have a well-choreographed hair flip. I told Kristin, "Band Research - wear fringe on stage." Chloe had on maroon tights, high-waisted white shorts and a crop top that was half tassel. Every time she did her be-pop/punk rock moves, it shook adorably.

The second act was a reggae band we had seen before as well, also envying their talent and stage presence. The lead singer is about five feet tall and double the stature, a Rasta prophet who between songs, tells us we are All One, and All Love. His hair had dreaded nicely since we saw him last. This time I noticed (because I am noticing these things now) that just like Sarah T. (leader of the Spread Eagles, who on this very stage, first rocked my world), he did not look at the audience once. He looked up toward the ceiling, as if communing with Jah himself (Sarah T.'s gaze was a bit more internal). Kristin, not performing, was on her second beer and danced so invitingly, a shy woman came up and asked if she could join. When the reggae wonder did Bob Marley's "One Love," I put aside my pre-performance jitters and boogied as well.

And then suddenly, it was my turn. That moment of stepping on stage is like the moment before bungee jumping, so glad you are finally doing it and so scared you are finally doing it. Fortunately I had a focal point - Kristin, who had moved a chair three feet from the stage and pantomimed how amazing I was doing. She also held up my iPhone and filmed the whole set.

Why It Was Successful:

1. I was prepared.
2. It was a manageable step.
3. I was surrounded by people who wanted me to succeed.
4. It was dark and noisy.

Some Things I Learned:

1. It was okay I did not invite/allow my boyfriend to watch me this first time, even though ironically, he was in town on a Friday night (which he hadn't been in months, as he usually has his kids up in Seattle). I have a very feminine habit of focusing all my attention on the man I am with and I didn't want the extra nervousness of messing up in front of the man I hope will someday be my hubby. Not yet.
2. It was fine no one was really listening. Actually, a few people did. Kelsey's dad had been hoping to hear me sing and I'd told him tonight was the night. He and his wife stuck around to do so.
3. The person recording your set probably shouldn't sing along with you, as their voice will be picked up louder, even

though you are amplified; they are one foot, not three feet from the microphone (Kristin sounded good though).

4. Sometimes just doing it is the thing. I got through and actually had fun. I especially loved Mark and Skyler backing me up.

5. There have been watershed moments in my life: being born, saying "I do," birthing four babies, adopting my boys from Ethiopia, meeting my current boyfriend, meeting a handful of amazing women friends AND making it through my first bonafide performance. It was that big. I broke through to a larger sense of who I am and what is possible for me. The best encore I could imagine.

A Second Chance at a Dream
by Kristin

In college I liked to smoke dope, so much, that it interfered with my dreams. One of those was to be a disc jockey on campus at our local radio station. I went so far as to apply and study, but on the day of my DJ test I was high, and inevitably ended up failing because I had too much "dead air." A perfect term for the spacey way pot could sometimes make me feel and act. In the DJ world, this is suicide. I have never gotten over that incident and even though I still want to DJ parties, I have never tried again.

Recently, almost twenty years later, I finally had the opportunity. My older son, Coletrane, turned seven and wanted a party that was unique, he asked me to come up with an idea. Cole is very much into dancing, learning hip hop moves and memorizing songs (a true mini-me). I woke up in the middle of the night with a fantastic idea - I would play DJ at his little kid party! He was all over it.

On the day of the party, I took an iPod with Cole's favorite songs and put it in the player, hooked up a microphone and set up chairs. When it was time for the festivities, I announced, "Hip hop Musical Chairs!!" I got the audience (the parents) jazzed by waving my hands, dancing and calling out each child in a cheerleader-like way.

Usually, I embarrass Coletrane with my gregariousness, but it worked in this scenario. The youngest participant, Elijah, was two and so his papa carried him joyfully around the circle.

When the music stopped, Elijah let out a delighted scream that galvanized the other kids to sing along and pay attention to the game.

From time to time, I looked over at my husband, Michael, who shook his head at me insinuating, "You are off your rocker, and I love you!" Sometimes my extroverted nature collides with his introverted personality and I can sense he wants me to calm down. Not today.

One of my goals for Violet has been to offer a dance party experience. This little baby step, DJ'ing for almost babies, helped me feel the original impetus for my dreams. Although I still lack some confidence, I am ready to polish my skill set - this time no pot, just lovely live air.

Carmen's Class Act
by Deborah

My second "gig" was appearing with Mark at the community college class, The History of Rock 'n' Roll, taught by Carmen Hoover, one of the women in my literature group. Carmen has been teaching this popular class for years, a retrospective studying music from the 1850's to present time. Every session she invites three bands to perform a set and be interviewed by her students, each segment running about forty-five minutes long. Carmen was short a band and asked a few months back what Violet was up to.

A whole lot of nada at that point, but I was studying away with Mark and felt that he and I could help, if she understood I was still learning. Carmen was excited about an "in process" experience and we were added to the class list. It was the perfect goal for me. Six songs memorized, supported by Mark. We worked out a list of slow and fast, new and old songs, throwing in one Prince hit as a nod to Carmen, who is a diehard fan. She actually lived in Minneapolis and had the pleasure of working on his first movie, *Purple Rain.*

Our set list was as follows in this order:

Sweet Child O' Mine, Guns 'n' Roses
Helpless, Neil Young
Down on the Corner, Credence Clearwater Revival
Can't Let Go, Lucinda Williams
Love Is What I Got, Sublime
When Doves Cry, Prince

Mark and I arrived early on a gorgeous day in Shelton at the Olympic Community College, about half an hour outside of Olympia. Neither one of us had ever been to the campus and were surprised to find it inspirational. Set among pines and rushes, it is a sacred space with open windows, art everywhere and a cozy student lounge. "Small is good in education" I have heard Carmen state and being in her stomping ground, I could see why. Carmen had some of her students as greeters there to help us unload our equipment. We had two acoustic guitars (that could be plugged in and amplified), microphones with stands, a mixing board and a speaker. Some other students were our official hosts; they asked if we needed anything and introduced us to the class, gave us thank you cards at the end that had been signed by each student. I decided then and there what I had already suspected - that Carmen should rule the world: it would be a smart, gentle, fun, well-run place, completely inclusive of all.

The group was an eclectic mix of young and older students. I immediately lit on a kid in the front with cerebral palsy, wearing a Sheryl Crow t-shirt and a purple scarf around his neck, a beautiful spunky girl off to the right, and an older student who had a Dave Matthew's vibe in the back. They seemed interested the entire time, a nice contrast to a clutch of girls seated dead center, who didn't smile once.

Mark and I bordered on old-fogeyness a few times, lecturing students to follow their dreams and why bands such as Creedence Clearwater were important, but overall, I feel we were genuine and interesting. Most wonderfully, I didn't mess up. Not once. Even though we were afraid we wouldn't have enough songs, turned out we had too many. Better problem to have.

The students had prepared questions. I wish I had known ahead of time so I could have given more inspired answers. They asked, "If you could have lunch with three people, living or dead, who would you choose?" I answered Maya Angelou, Sheryl Crow and Gandhi. In hindsight I would swap out G-man for Eve Ensler, the creator of the *Vagina Monologues*. I was asked what my family thought of my playing music (I answered, "approvals all around"), what we thought of dubstep techno music ("not my fave, prefer live music any day, but it has its place and I can't help but dance to it"). The questions were thoughtful and thought-provoking. We finished with our present to Carmen, our cover of Prince's "When Doves Cry." Mark was happy, Carmen was happy. I was thrilled.

Afterwards, I stopped at a convenience store and bought some junk food, then met my boyfriend for a smooch. I could see why musicians have reputations for partying and philandering, I was high on adrenaline. My version of sex 'n' drugs after rock 'n' roll - barbecue potato chips, M&M's and making out in a car. Never better.

"What Kind of Music Do You Play?"
by Rain

It's the first question out of everyone's mouth when they find out we're in a band, and the hardest to answer. A year ago, I would toss off a cheery "Soul Glam!" in response. I was all about Bowie and T-Rex, Deborah brought in Chaka Khan and Michael Franti, and Kristin added Regina Spector and Stevie Wonder to the cauldron. How's that for a melting pot?

The fact that we were rank newbies at our instruments forced us into a stripped-down style that we soon found we liked. Whittling down allowed the bones of the song to show through. Learning to play from scratch meant slowing down the faster songs, which let the words take center stage. We became more selective in our song choices. Were these lyrics we could put our souls into, month after month? Were they, god forbid, both universal and personal? A neat trick, if you can manage it.

So. A guitar, drums, a lead singer, a backup singer (Kristin being on hiatus from the band). What could we conjure up with such minimal elements? What inspired us? And most of all, what gave us full-body goosebumps, those precursors to *transcendence*. Which is, after all, our band's credo, or at least the password we chose for our first email account, even if it IS so damn hard to spell. We gravitated to songs like "Second Hand News" and "I Want to Hold Your Hand," tried and true chestnuts that held unexpected nuance. And "Back on the Chain Gang," certainly a feeling most of us can identify with, especially come Monday morning. Gut-wrenchers like Lucinda

Williams' "Can't Let Go" and Patty Griffin's "Mad Mission" helped us in our muddle through that thing called love. Although I had written a handful of songs, and Deborah oodles of poetry, we felt content to copy the masters for now.

What was this sound we were cultivating? Indie rock? Such a massive category as to be almost meaningless. Americana? Not really. Between us, we'd traveled the world. R&B? What genre could describe a couple of chicks sitting around, coaxing thoughts and feelings from our throats and limbs?

Deborah kept the bar held high, refusing anything glossy or over-produced. Glam fell by the wayside as we embraced Scout Niblett's and rapper Macklemore's idiosyncratic approaches. We dug deep to find those rough, ragged bits in ourselves to share. I curled up with the Stones on my iPod. Nobody does fierce, impassioned background vocals better than Keith Richards. We searched around for templates to mold ourselves to, from Janis Joplin and Shannon Hoon to Tom Waits. Those who had the courage to just be themselves. Nothing's more beautiful than that.

Then it came to me... we sing SOAK music! Soul plus folk! Music you can strip down and ease into like a hot springs spa. Music that makes you feel good, that is uplifting, healing and still very real. That evokes the feeling you get when you soak in something, or soak something in - be it knowledge, beauty or simply sound.

Summer of Slack or How to Make a Violet Vixen
by Deborah

I recently staged a photo shoot, my subject was so gorgeous I couldn't resist. Not a musician or even a person, I clicked away at a picture of a cocktail, a purple slurple I made for Rain and Kristin. It seemed to be the crowning achievement of Violet the band this summer. The drink is a yummy concoction of:

Santa Cruz organic limeade
vodka*
a dollop of Dreyer's BlackBerry ice cream **
lots of ice
a violet ***

* any vodka will do, but we have found the better the booze, the less regret the next morning... Grey Goose (if we are feeling French) or DryFly (local yumminess, made in eastern Washington) are staples in my freezer

** sherbet would work, but somehow the creaminess of this ice cream was wonderful

*** which we didn't have at the time, but plan to have next time, they are edible you know...

What wasn't pictured in my kitchen were the ten children that were happily running around, jumping on the trampoline, riding the four-wheeler and karaoke-ing in the music room. With no nannies this summer (not that there ever were, and actually Rain was a nanny to four extra children) and only one soccer camp for my boisterous boys, Violet barely lifted an instrument, let alone made any progress.

It felt like time to be fallow, to chill, to front-load the kids with attention. There were big changes this fall for everyone (of the ten Violet progeny, seven of them started new schools) and it seemed everyone just needed to BE. For my crew, we let everything go - no tennis or music lessons, no seven-hundred-mile trip to Grandma's house. The major accomplishments were a few of my boys landing front flips on the trampoline. Rain, Kristin and I even found we weren't listening to music as much, letting even that well run dry.

One Day, In Teletubby Land
by Rain

Today I nannied for fifteen straight hours. All four of my part-time charges ended up coming on the same day, a "perfect storm" of nannying. While feeding and wiping them, I also pottied the puppy repeatedly and took my eldest daughter to and from ballet classes. In and out, shoes on, shoes off, leash on, leash off, swing, teeter-totter, play-doh, wash hands, diaper change ("Legs still, please!" through clenched teeth), Top Ramen all around, juice, *sshh* nap, where are your football pants, banana handout, don't run through the flowers!

I do love children; they are so full of green, growing life. But if they were my only occupation, I'd stick a diaper pin through my heart and end it all right now. I need a part of my existence that is wild, that is a frontier town, where I am not always in charge, and where the surprises don't usually involve poop. I need to traipse barefoot through the fields, and not just after a vanishing toddler. Otherwise, I start feeling drab, drab, drab. Did I mention drab? *Faded and dull in appearance; of a common place character; dreary.* Drab.

That's where the band comes to the rescue. All day, as I kiss boo-boos and peel peaches, I let the back of my mind linger on Violet, and feel the cool rush of the magical unknown. A simple text from Deborah reminds me of my other self: *Squeeze in some practice time later, Petal?* I love everything about being in a band - meeting for practice, picking songs to cover, learning new rhythms, seeing my bandmates stretch and grow, feeling myself do the same. Watching our style evolve organically. And of course, picking out fabulous outfits to wear, ones that don't have gooey fingerprints trekking across them.

At the start of practice, I pull out my musical notations, much scratched out and re-written, re-arrange the drum kit lefty-style, and try an exploratory snare drum riff: *rat-a-tat*. Each drum set has a slightly different sound and feel. I adjust myself to it, whether it is at our local school of rock, in Deborah's music room, or in my own garage. I look around. Everyone else is plugging in their instruments and tuning up. There are no windows, no distractions in the rehearsal room. The energy is curiously telescoped and concentrated, yet relaxed.

I love to think how all of my musical heroes went through precisely these same steps each time they started work. The ritual is delicately intoxicating, like a Japanese tea ceremony. More than playing notes, we are here to capture the elusive groove. And definitely, definitely - to run through the flowers!

When the last mother rings the doorbell and her boys barrel out toward her minivan, she tosses a wistful question over her shoulder at me: "How's the band?" I know her job as a nurse involves long hours of caring for others, too. I wonder if she is able to carve out time in her crowded schedule for that all-important "me time," for something that makes her light up within. I hope so. "The band is doing great," I answered. "Really great."

Even her nine-year-old son surprised me today by asking, "How many other people are in your band?" All of the children have had a good bash on my drum set. My identity as a musician, so laborious for me to assume, seems an easy fit for others. They reflect it back to me, and help me grow into it.

Amy Winehouse RIP
by Rain

Singer/songwriter Amy Winehouse died a week ago. As we await toxicology reports, the assumption is that, if drugs and alcohol didn't outright kill her, they certainly contributed to her death. I confess I was not familiar with her music, but had always enjoyed her fully-formed style aesthetic when I came across her picture in magazines. With her wings of black eyeliner and her sky-high beehive, her look was bold, irreverent and above all, fun.

Turns out the petite chanteuse won five Grammy awards in 2008, including Best New Artist. Her blend of jazz, blues and soul was credited with re-invigorating the British music industry. She co-wrote her songs, and her distinctive contralto vocals were compared to Billie Holiday and Aretha Franklin. Following her success, record executives sought out fearless and experimental female musicians, giving rise to such talents as Lady Gaga, Adele, and Florence and the Machine.

Winehouse was a tabloid regular for her tempestuous relationship with then-husband Blake Fielder-Civil, who reputedly introduced her to crack cocaine and heroin. Her final performances in Belgrade are sadly disoriented. She wanders the stage aimlessly, scratching her arms and forgetting half the lyrics. The tour was abruptly canceled and she flew home. In several interviews, Winehouse revealed she was bi-polar, a condition difficult to manage under the best of circumstances. Especially so in a culture that has little understanding and tolerance for mental "illness" or other-ness.

Winehouse now joins the "27 Club" - musicians like Janis Joplin, Jim Morrison, Jimi Hendrix and Kurt Cobain, who passed from this world at that age. Honorary members must include twenty-eight-year-old Blind Melon frontman, Shannon Hoon, and twenty-six-year-old Nick Drake. You will find all of these artists were not only musicians, but quite amazing visionaries, painters, sculptors, poets, and designers. Each of them propelled the popular art of their day into fresh fields of discovery.

I like to think of these artists as shooting stars, whose luminescent streak through life causes us to catch our breath in awe. Being born with so much creativity must be like being issued a wild mustang and being forced to train it while riding at galloping speed. Exhilarating, but damn near impossible. The fickle fulcrum of fame turns the pressure up even higher.

If you believe that this world is all we have, then, yes, an early death is tragic. But if you believe we are all essentially spiritual beings, then death has to be a welcome return to Source, to the larger part of ourselves. After all, how many cheese sandwiches can you eat in a lifetime? How many years spent trotting out your hits in casino after casino? In my mind, I see Amy joining the others in a castle of clouds and being offered a canape and a silken cushion to recline on. As these bright souls rest up for their next adventure, we can take sustenance from the treasures they left behind: their songs, their passion - their raw love.

Sweetly Stung
by Deborah

I once asked my beau, "If you could be any performer, who would you be?" He didn't hesitate to answer Sting. It seemed fitting when I found out Sting was coming to Seattle, to get tickets and give them to my guy for his birthday. I didn't have the tickets yet when his actual b-day dawned, so I found a card with a dog playing a guitar and printed out some Sting images and pasted them in. I also wrapped a few pairs of binoculars and a packet of Kleenex (for nosebleed seating).

The concert was almost a month after his birthday and two days before mine, so we made it a joint celebration. The Paramount Theatre is festive as a cake, a gilded affair with balcony upon balcony of velvet and gold. We were about as high up as you can get, anyone with vertigo or fear of heights might have had a hard time with the seventy-degree pitch.

Sting is a musician's musician and a songwriter as well. I had read that for his last tour, he had a forty-eight piece symphony accompany him. This tour he was calling, "Back to Bass." Sting is one of the few lead singers who plays bass guitar. He had two other guitarists, and two violin/fiddle players; one of the violin players was the only girl on the tour and also did backup vocals, a lovely Australian named Jo Lawry.

First off, Sting looked damn good. Well, actually, I couldn't really see him, as we forgot the binoculars, but I could tell his body was toned and agile at sixty, with the nicely sculpted arms of someone who has been packing an electric guitar for forty-five years. Secondly, his voice filled the theatre, every filigreed detail, every cell of the thousand people watching. He sounded better live than on any recording and sang for two straight hours; most performers half his age struggle to accomplish that. Sting was wonderfully generous with the spotlight, offered it up on many occasions to his other bandmates. His lead guitarist stepped forward with his grown son, a fiddler, and played a long solo, while Sting retreated to the dark, watching this family duo with reverence.

He chatted between songs, giving us background and a sense of what matters to him - silence as well as music, family and his fans. We were surprised that he has written some country songs: "I'm So Happy That I Can't Stop Crying" was made a hit by Toby Keith. He writes songs like I do poems - telling stories in prose. My favorite was "Stolen Car (Take Me Dancing)," the story of a thief who once in a stolen ride, absorbs the life of the man who owned the car. In the song, his wife and mistress both ask him to take them dancing. As his backup singer wailed, "Take me dancing," I felt the sorrow of the infidelity I have had in my own life.

As a segue to one of his love songs, he said people always acted like his marriage of thirty-two years to his wife, Trudie, was a miracle. He said, "That woman healed me and filled in the holes in my soul - she also has the power to completely devastate me." My beau held on tight during those words. I wanted to personally thank Sting, as I feel in my relationship, I have healed and been healed. Seems I wasn't the only woman who paid attention to this comment: a female reviewer wrote,

"Another nice moment was when Sting explained how he'd been with his wife Trudie for thirty-two years and that she saved him and he saved her, but that marriage takes work (elbow nudge to my husband)."

Sting did perform his gold standards - "Every Breath You Take," "Every Little Thing She Does is Magic" and my favorite of all time, "Fields of Gold," although I was quite disappointed he did not do "Love Is the Seventh Wave." He had three encores; for the final one, he came out solo and played "Message In a Bottle," accompanying himself on a ukelele. Finally, everyone in the band came out and took a bow holding hands, then walked off without fanfare. Sting, born Gordon Sumner, stayed true to his humble roots - son of a common man from England, who for a time when he was young wore a scarf with black and yellow stripes, hence the stage name.

This concert marked a turning point in my appreciation for music that I owe to Violet. I had hoped to have a nice time as I liked Sting enough, had even seen him with the Police when I was a teenager, but I predicted my enjoyment would be primarily witnessing my boyfriend's joy. What I found was I experienced the concert on many levels, most of them new to me. I was intrigued by the band's chemistry, the choice and order of the songs, the pacing of the concert. Having attempted to perform, I was in awe of a flawless two-hour production. I valued the breadth of Sting's career. I felt like a true connoisseur, as my musical palate is educated, my pleasure is expanded.

You Can Do Magic
by Rain

"Mom, the tickets are selling fast!" My eleven-year-old daughter's eyes were pleading. Selena Gomez, her personal pop princess, was coming to the county fair.

I recognized the longing behind that look. I'd had the same look, I'm sure, when I was fourteen. Cliff Richard, my personal pop prince, was making the trek from Great Britain to Wellington, New Zealand, where I lived, and performing at a downtown theater. He had glossy black hair, spaniel eyes, and Chiclet teeth. I HAD to go. I loved his music. Plus, it was my secret ambition to marry him.

My understanding mother bought me a ticket and dropped me at the theater. I went alone, feeling very grown-up. It was glorious. The theater was a rococo wonder, with balconies galore. Cliff sang all of his hits ("Summer Holiday," anyone?), his music a brand of sugary pop that would make my teeth ache today. He changed outfits not one, but four times. His three-piece white suit, in particular, is seared across my brain. Afterwards, we got engaged. Just kidding.

So when Selena beckoned, we followed; a simple click of the mouse bought us five tickets. We wrangled another mother and two of my daughter's friends into coming with us. I felt flattered that my daughter wanted me to join her.

Existential Question: Are you or are you not the type of parent who lets her middle-schooler go to a concert on a school night? I think we all know I am.

The fairgrounds were teeming with bedazzled tweenagers and their slightly frazzled parents. We found our seats on the concrete bleachers, about halfway up. Flanking the stage were two massive video screens, so everyone had a great view of the action. After a suitable period of anticipation, the three-piece band and two backup singers took their places. Suddenly, Selena herself was skipping across the stage, launching into her hits, "A Year Without Rain" and "Who Says." She had glossy black hair, spaniel eyes and Chiclet teeth. Deja vu. She frolicked, she grinned, she flipped her hair. Her voice was strong and supple, her songs teetering between solid and bubblegum pop.

I was impressed that she didn't hide behind florid production values, auto-tune devices, and the various other smoke and mirrors available to today's pop tarts. Everywhere, girls were on their feet, squealing, dancing and singing along. I'm pretty sure my daughter was the loudest (her neon-green outfit definitely was). Selena's positivity was infectious. "Don't ever let anyone tell you you can't do something," she counseled before singing "Tell Me Something I Don't Know." "I'm here on this stage because all of you believed in me. I remember going to my first concert when I was thirteen. I saw Britney Spears! It was amazing."

With a poof of confetti, the concert was over. We trucked past a long line of people waiting to purchase Selena merchandise. "Buy it on eBay," my practical daughter suggested, as we headed for the curly fries stand. We strolled right by booths touting Vitamix blenders, cut-rate insurance plans and hand-painted signs of *Love Grown Here*. We were satiated. We had what we came for. As Selena's encore song, "You Can Do Magic," and Cliff Richard's song from all those years ago reminded us: you can have what you desire, and life can be like a summer holiday. Including, especially, first concert experiences. A rite of passage, and a bit of enchantment, for us all.

No Shit, No Violets
by Deborah

Another typical Friday night found me cavorting with fabulous, inspiring musicians. Well, I was watching them on YouTube, but it was still fabulous and inspiring, so much so I was still referencing the things I heard and saw weeks later. Rain calls them bunnyholes or wormholes. They go something like this - at nine p.m. you decide to look up just one song on YouTube, and at eleven, you have cried twice, printed out the chords to three songs and recommitted to being a musician. YouTube for a musician is Las Vegas for a gambler, without the bankruptcy and hangover. For the phrase above (which has become my personal mantra for getting through tough times) I thank the following worms or bunnies - Van Morrison, Eddie Vedder and Glen Hansard.

I was researching "Into the Mystic" by Van Morrison after attempting to play it. YouTube highlighted him singing this song during the span of three decades: from shagginess to a comb-over to baldness, starting and ending with polyester. I then watched others cover the song, finding among the amateurs singing in their bathrooms (that and empty garages, good acoustics), Glen Hansard. Hansard is a musician who won the Oscar for his song, "Falling Slowly," done with Marketa Iglova in 2008. He was "busking" Morrison's hit on a street corner in a busy city.

"Busking" is a new term for me: *when one sings in public for voluntary donations*. I watched Glen cover many songs, sometimes garnering attention and other times not. Finally, I watched him sing his seminal hit, "Falling Slowly," the song that catapulted him from a guy busking to performing at music festivals all over the country. He was joined by such creme-de-la-creme musicians as Eddie Vedder, the lead singer of Pearl Jam. Eddie Vedder backed up Glen, his harmonies flawless and full of feeling. Glen introduced his famous song after telling a story about overcoming hardship, with which he illustrated the moral, *No shit, no roses.*

Probably not original to him, but those four words bring light to all the suffering and unwelcome crap in our lives. If I look back on Violet's collective month, we have had a romantic break-up, a mental breakdown, the flu, money issues, all punctuated by the usual kid drama. Out of the compost, shoots have sprung: we came up with the byline for Kristin's memoir about overcoming depression, Rain turned her blonde mane (which was feeling like straw) into a tawny sleek do, the kids seem to miraculously be doing okay and spring has finally arrived in the Northwest, roses and violets imminent.

Birthday a'billy!
by Kristin

To celebrate my last year in my thirties, a decade in which I got married, relocated from California to Washington, created a family and finally learned to let go of what anyone thinks about me, I gathered all my friends and had a band play in my honor at the Robin Hood Restaurant in Union. As I got dressed in a hot pink dress, fishnet stockings, violet seahorse earrings and my Brazilian cowgirl boots, I was excited to have a convergence of so many people I love. Deborah, Rain and my dad were driving up from Olympia and I had my wonderful Union posse.

The featured band, Angie and The Car Wrecks, showed up to give the audience a taste of what rockabilly is all about. They play the upright bass, rhythm guitar, lead guitar and the washboard. The band consists of Angie and Dale, who are married, and Angie's brother, Shawn, who started playing the bass (named Alvira) because he won a coin toss with Dale. I was invited to touch and strum Alvira during the intermission. Her power enveloped me, the size and strength creating such presence, I had a hard time parting with her. I can see why Alvira was won by lady luck!

The pub was packed. I enjoyed a special drink called the Dizzler, named appropriately, because too many and you became quite dizzy. I looked around the dance floor and saw Rain and her beau watching me with mirth and laughter in their eyes. The drink came to my rescue moments later when I was twirled around by a friend. As I went under his arm, my right shoulder popped out of its socket. Luckily the Dizzler saved the day and I felt no pain as I popped it back in. I didn't miss a beat.

My papa was in a celebratory mood as well, every time I looked over he was regaling one of my hot friends with a story. He had them hanging on his every word, good ol' pops.

I was interested in the lead singer Angie, the only woman in the band, because we shared the same influences - Joan Jett and Pat Benatar, my role models growing up. My mom is also a huge fan - we spent summers driving to Cape Cod, their music pumping through the open windows. I remember the artists' jet black hair. Angie was as bold, with blond and ebony two-toned locks, bright red lipstick and a sizzlin' outfit. No one would guess that by day she is studying to be a nurse, hospital scrubs are hard to imagine on this songbird (although if I was choking I would love her lips to be on mine).

Dale, Angie's husband, is another story altogether. I enjoyed his website bio, where he is said to like frivolous women and alcohol, my kind of guy. He and I share a commonality (not frivolous women!) but our desire to change instruments. He used to play the electric bass, but when his interest fizzled, he picked up the lead guitar and has been at it for thirteen years. This inspired me, as I have flirted with the harmonica, keyboard and now, bass guitar.

The washboard that Pigpen played seemed to hold it all together, its "zzz, zzz, zzz" sound made me stomp my feet, hoot and holler. Pigpen had great facial expressions that matched the various sounds. I immediately added washboard to my wish list. The Car Wrecks played some originals, but by far the most loved songs were by Johnny Cash. I had never enjoyed his music before, but now I have a new appreciation. I have since listened to "Walk the Line" many times while cleaning my house, it is catchy as hell, I see why the audience ate it up. Like Cash, I plan on keeping a close eye on this heart o' mine in the coming decade, with gratitude for the circle of friendship it has brought me.

Slow Hand
by Deborah

We had just got back with Skyler for instruction, and then subsequently cancelled the next few months. We seem to be in a Catch-22, thinking we need to practice to earn our session, or be worthy of it, then not practicing because we don't have the pressure of an upcoming lesson.

Here is what I am realizing - you are a musician if you make music. Period. In the same vein, you are a writer if you write. I have been worrying if we are good or bad, talented or not. The real question is, are we playing? It's been a month since I touched my guitar. It got so out of tune, I couldn't get it back, even with my electric tuner (I broke a string once when it was this far gone and am terrified to have that happen again). My human tuner (my oldest son) just moved out. So, I have had my unplayable Arbor in the back of my minivan for three weeks, hoping to get to the music store for a free tweak.

Last time we were with Skyler, he said, "When you don't know how to do something, do it really slowly." Well, the whole process of being a band has been slower than any of us would like. The old ten percent inspiration, ninety percent perspiration adage. Even two hundred percent inspiration does not a band make.

The thing is, even when we play something we know, slow is fitting our aesthetic right now. When we started Violet, we envisioned an alternative to the dance club we liked to go to. We wanted to play covers that got people off their feet and moving. The metronome for most of the hits we have been attempting is set at about 140-150 beats per minute, we are now easing it down to 80-90.

For a few reasons. One, so I can get the chord changes in there, but more importantly, because we are choosing songs we love the lyrics of; we are wordsmiths first. We had chosen "Second Hand News" by Fleetwood Mac, thinking finally we'd throw in a fast one. Three attempts in, I said, "Rain, let's try the first verse a cappella, add chords the second and drums on the chorus." We know we are on the right track when one or more of us gets goosebumps. Well we did, harmonizing on the simply wonderful lines that speak to us about laying down in tall grass, and doing our "stuff."

Eric Clapton is famously nicknamed Slow Hand; he is anything but. According to Wikipedia, the nickname began when he played in England with the Yardbirds and would stay onstage to change a broken string. The audiences would wait out the delay with a "slow handclap." In Clapton's biography, it is said that the nickname evolved care of Giorgio Gomelsky, who coined it as a play on words because Clapton's jamming was so fast.

I have known all along that I lack several key ingredients to become a Clapton copycat - youth, talent and time among them. Even though Clapton's nickname came from his speed, I like to think it also came from his willingness to slow down and learn, which he did when he was young, watching the blues masters. And when Clapton did slow and strip down later in his career, letting his voice shine on his 1992 album, *Unplugged*, people noticed. In fact, it is his best-selling work. We are joking our byline can be, "We play covers, just half as fast!" What we are finding is our truest expression, slow hands for lots of reasons, in good company.

AMERICA'S GOT TALENT (?)
BY RAIN

Free tickets! The news that free tickets were available online to watch Seattle's auditions for the TV show *America's Got Talent* spread through my daughter's school like lice. And so it was that I found myself with five girls, and one other game mom, in an SUV on the freeway. If you don't count the $26 parking garage fee, the $160 restaurant tab, and the $20 monorail jaunt, it was TOTALLY FREE.

Does Seattle have talent? Visions of Nirvana, Pearl Jam and Jimi Hendrix pirouetted in my head. Here we were at ground zero, about to witness the latest local sensation. The fact that none of those artists would've been caught dead on a cheesy show like AGT blissfully did not enter my head, filled as it was with rainbows, cotton candy and Stratocasters.

We did the obligatory peasants-standing-curbside-in-the-freezing-drizzle thing, which sounds like more fun than it actually is. Periodically a limo would pull up, and the crowd would erupt in pealing squeals of pent-up longing. Our girls would dart like Dickensian urchins to the street and report breathlessly back to us.
"It's Nick Cannon!!" I tried to look like I knew (and cared) who that was.
"It's the host!"
"Oh, wow!" I attempted.
"He's wearing a GREEN JACKET!!"
"Awesome!"

Finally, we were herded into the Paramount Theatre and strip-searched... I mean, metal-detector-ed by security staff bent on separating us from our cameras and cell phones (aka our umbilical cords). We found seats in the balcony from which, if we stood on tiptoe and craned our necks, we still couldn't see the fabulously famous judges - Howie Mandel (was I the only one old enough to remember him as a stand-up comic with a rubber glove on his now-bald head?), Sharon Osborne (did *she* ever take a career opportunity and run with it!) and Piers Somebody-Or-Other (from that hotbed of cultural cognizance, CNN).

People in black, with headsets, scurried back and forth across the stage like worker ants, and a man (dressed in black, with a headset) in Buddy Holly glasses began whipping the crowd into a frenzy worthy of the Roman Coliseum at its lusty peak. "Let's show some APPRECIATION!" Roar! "I wanna HEAR you, Seattle!" Squeal! Roar! He then flattered us absurdly to achieve those enthusiastic "cutaway" shots. "You are so much better than Portland was!" Roar! "*And* better-looking!" Squeal, roar, clap, whistle, stomp! I looked around at our pasty Northwest faces and generous thighs crammed into miniskirts. Shameless liar.

If you watch the show and a "cutaway" happens to show a blond woman shoving earplugs in her ears - that's me.

For the first act, an unprepossessing gentleman ambled onstage and explained that he was going to blow up a hot water bottle until it burst.

I would at this juncture like to note (and gently remind AGT scouts) that the *American Heritage Dictionary* defines talent as: *natural endowment or ability of a superior quality.* Nowhere does it mention hot water bottles. Not only that, but while the gentleman did in fact blow the bottle up until it was as large, and red, as himself, it did not burst. Perhaps it was the hot water bottle that was of superior quality, and not the talent.

He was followed by a bewildering array of more "talent," remarkable chiefly for its banality. There was a man who blew bubbles; I'm pretty sure I saw him at the public library once. A pair of zaftig "opera" singers, a faded stand-up comedian, some 90's-style break dancers and a chihuahua who pushed balls into the pockets of a pool table in no particular order. Yawn. When a sixty-nine-year-old tap dancer stepped onto the stage in silver hot pants, the high school girls behind me needed no help in providing their own pithy judgements: "This will scar me for life" and "This should not even be legal!"

The judges, bless 'em, were constructive in their criticism (all except Piers, a trigger-happy buzzer-pusher if there ever was one). Sharon encouraged everyone to work on the "entertainment value" of their acts, while Howie was positive though realistic in his assessments. Every ten minutes the cameras would stop, and make-up peons would powder the judges' noses while a grown man brought around drinks for them to sip. There's a stunning job in showbiz for you - Human Cup Holder. Meanwhile, Buddy Holly elicited impromptu performances from audience members, almost all of whom outshone the onstage acts.

By now, mob mentality had taken us by our throats, and bloodthirsty boos and cheers ricocheted off the intricately carved gilt ceiling, setting the chandeliers quaking. The image of Romans condemning their countrymen to death with down-turned thumbs swam before my eyes, and I hoped the contestants had a good hold of their livers.

Seattle, however, did not completely disgrace itself. An eleven-year-old girl tore into "Proud Mary" and if I were Rhianna, I'd start packing my bags. And four brothers called Boys Not Toys gave the Jonas Brothers a run for their money.

The most poignant moment came when a young man unicycled onstage. As Howie commented, "You're a juggler and yet I can't help notice you have only one arm."

"I lost my arm at age six, and ever since then I've had to prove I could do everything a two-armed person could do," the man replied.

Well, he started juggling balls, bowling balls, knives, ferrets (just kidding) and quickly proved he could do everything an eight-armed person could do. The crowd cheered, the judges beamed, and the juggler won the ultimate accolade - he gets to go on to the next round in... Las Vegas!

But not me. Not even for free.

A Trip to Tori Land
by Kristin

I had just gotten home from a particularly grueling morning
and when I walked into the house, my husband Michael was
prattling on about what our older son Coletrane had done to
make him crazy while I was gone. The complaints and the
never-ending days of gray and rain had me in no mood to hear
any of it. I turned away and then, in mid-sentence, Michael
switched gears and said with nonchalance, " Oh shit, your dad
called a few hours ago and said something about his date
bailing for the Tori Amos show tonight in Seattle." I stopped
cleaning the kitchen and mouthed the words, "A dream come
true," to no one in particular. I panted as I dialed my dad's
number, hoping I was not too late, as I have a sister who also
gets asked to his last-minute rendezvous. That's our dad for
you. Luckily he had not yet phoned her.

I had not explored Seattle since my pregnant days with Azure,
who is now almost five. I got dolled up and walked into my
papa's house. Dad has not seen me out of a t-shirt in ages and
was quite tickled to see his daughter ready for an adult
adventure! We started our odyssey at The Dragon Fish Cafe
where a sparkly waitress brought us sake and informed us that
it was ladies' night. All around us goddesses flitted about while
I stayed planted and consumed huge quantities of seaweed and
sushi. Finally it was time to go find Rain and Deborah at the
theater. I had known they would be there celebrating their
December birthdays and I was thrilled to be able to join them.

I discovered Miss Amos in college, when the pack of girls I hung out with sang her songs during many an occasion. The last school memory I have is of the four of us young lasses in a forbidden jacuzzi listening to "Cornflake Girl." College was a highlight of my life and to know that the songs I would hear tonight, could transport me back in time, was almost too much for me. The chandelier dimmed and I brightened.

Tori came out in a flowing diaphanous shirt, a pair of green culottes and razor-sharp stilettos, an outfit I never would have put together but homegirl had it goin' on! She had her band with her during the first part of her show. There was a cohesiveness on stage I would love to achieve with Violet. I imagine the musicians could have closed their eyes for the entire concert and played just as well together. I felt the audience open their hearts - unadulterated bliss.

Tori straddled her piano bench while playing her piano and an electronic keyboard simultaneously. She precariously balanced on a stiletto heel while her bench seemed to float, giving the effect that she was riding a beautiful horse. Her band, consisting of four young men, heartily played their violins and cellos to create unique backdrops to her devastating vocals. The light show, complete with swirly stars and flashes of clear light against the dark drapery completed "Tori Land." Tori's songs are haunting and full of messages of personal empowerment. She has taken tragedy and given it vivid imagery that lifts the veils of illusion. I looked over at my dad, he had his eyes closed, a huge grin and his hands were softly tapping on his pants. This was my favorite part of the night. This image will always remind me of his dedication to bring music into my life.

Tori, Almost
by Deborah

It was the concert of the year - one of our newly favorite singers at the elegant Paramount Theatre in Seattle, smack in the middle of Rain and my Sagittarian birthdays. Rain dressed like an ivory fairy goddess: layer upon layer of creams and ruffles atop pale tights and a paler miniskirt. I had on a dark dress with a jewel-bedazzled neckline and my favorite Marshall's find - a forest green pleather jacket with Michael Jackson-style zippers. "Yin and Yang" we proclaimed, and were off, over the wet freeways, through Seattle's convention center labyrinth to the glamor of the Paramount. We arrived just in time to try their specialty drink, named "Cornflake Girl" in honor of Tori, a vodka and cranberry concoction, wonderfully our cocktail of choice. I downed two quickly. More importantly, just in time to hobnob with Kristin who was there with her dad. She looked fabulous wearing a vanilla crochet top with a stunning pendant (a plastic cheapy purchased at Goodwill for a Halloween costume that looked better than the Hope Diamond). Something about throwing back vodka makes me say the "f" word a lot, and for five minutes, I was on f'ing fire.

Our seats weren't bad, Kristin's even not-badder. Rain and I settled in, a snuck-in bag of barbecue chips included, ready to be dazzled. We were definitely among the most rocker-ed out chicks: our seat mates on either side smelled (stale cigarettes and greasy food) and looked (sweat pants and faded worn sweaters) like they belonged at a movie matinee rather than a concert. The opening duo Rain quickly dubbed "straight out of Oly" and she was right - two very sweet, self-effacing dudes, a Kenny

Loggins look-alike playing acoustic guitar and singing, accompanied by a Kelsey Grammar doppelganger with a zither. The lead guy kept thanking us for being there and saying "Wow, you guys are great," which was kind, but became annoying. I prefer a little ego with my lead males.

I was intrigued by the zither, had never seen one front and center, usually they are the sixth, not the second guitar in a gig, played by a guy behind an amp. I asked Rain if she'd ever consider trying one, to which she snorted, "Never." I told her for her seventieth birthday I'd give her one, it would be a welcome relief from drumming for her, by that point, arthritic elbows. She said she'd throw it at me. We happily ate our chips when the audience clapped.

The set was the same black backdrop I had seen a week before when I'd gone to see Sting. Tonight, instead of the usual rock band set up, there was a Bösendorfer grand piano under a chandelier whose LED lights flickered post-modernly. Tori came out to enthusiastic, yet respectful applause wearing a silver ninja/space tunic, with two gray pieces of fabric sewn across her left shoulder, creating a sort of gypsy flag. The tunic was worn over a pair of sky-blue capris which showed off her spray-tanned ankles and bright blue, patent stiletto pumps. Her trademark thin hair was suspiciously thick, auburn curls fell down to the middle of her back. She said "Hello Seattle!" and mounted her piano bench in the characteristic pose she is famous for. We held our breath. We were so wanting to be amazed, so wanting to be touched. We had been concerned we wouldn't be.

Rain and I were rather new to Tori. As we began our Violet journey we discovered her memoir (at a thrift shop of course), which led us to her music. Her book, *Piece by Piece*, was an amalgamation of Wiccan practicum, confessional journaling, feminist theory and rock history. It was very authentic. We then listened to her music. I loved "Silent All These Years" and "A Sorta Fairytale," Rain liked "Tallulah." We both were super vodka-excited to hear "Cornflake Girl." Rain had also scored a VCR recording of Tori's music videos and had been appreciating them more every day for their surreal symbolism and creativity. She especially loved Tori's beautiful unique face and how her mouth expressed her emotions.

We were concerned because once the concert date approached, we began to study Tori more closely, finding she was famous for something other than her talent - hers was one of the first names to pop up on the "Twenty-five Worst Plastic Surgeries of All Time" websites. In horror, we scrolled to find before and after pictures of her, most commonly compared to a Smurf. Gone was the secret about her lips as if she'd just made love or wanted to, gone was the thin curly hair that looked just like mine, gone were her cheekbones. She looked swollen and strange. We felt ripped off and saddened and angry. In order to detox, I embarked on a non-plastic surgery quest, searching the internet for hours for images of women my age and older who had not significantly altered their face. Helen Mirren, Lauren Hutton, Meryl Streep, Julianne Moore, Liv Ullmann staring back at me with their wrinkles, consoled me. I took solace looking at singers like Sinead O' Connor and Melissa Etheridge, Joan Baez and Patti Smith.

Rain and I tried to love the concert and Tori. We tried hard. And then about halfway through we stopped trying. We were exasperated and bored. Instead of her usual band (a bass guitarist and drummer, both of whom had written about how amazing it was to play with Tori because they got to improvise and groove with her) she had a classical string quartet - two violins, a viola and a cello. Every song seemed to have the same pattern, the same feverish pitch three-quarters of the way in, strings sawing, Tori's fingers pounding. I imagine to those who knew every lyric, there was some variance, but to us newbies, it was monotonous.

Tori did not stray from her piano, did not patter between songs, let alone share their significance in her life. She played none of the three songs I liked, even though on iTunes they are her top sellers. The thing that did vary was the lights. Every song had a different color, about three effects were rotated. Her background boys (she called them the Fab Four which would offend any decent Beatle fan) all reminded me of Harry Potter (with similar dark clothes, long bangs and pale skin). With the chandelier and light show against the baroque architecture, I was reminded of a scene at Hogwarts, felt I was in the middle of *The Deathly Hollows* (speaking of plastic surgery, the last time I saw J.K. Rollins pitch her new interactive website, *Potterville*, she looked eerily like the American Idol singer, Carrie Underwood).

I wanted to break the violins in half. I wanted to hurl Rain's purse (a furry number, so that whenever she grabs her keys, I imagine her pulling out steaming entrails) and have it turn into a raccoon and attack Tori, rip her wig off. It was not just her face and hair that were askew. Her movements were contrived, she had no repartee with her audience, this from the woman who was legendary for connecting with her fans. Rain refused to use the binoculars we brought and laid back in her seat and closed her eyes. I emulated her, hoping it would help. Unfortunately it didn't.

In dissecting my distaste for Tori's new appearance, I tried to accept that certain artists enhance their looks to appeal to their audience. From the beginning of time, humans have adorned themselves. Someone could argue that a headdress is no different than a wig, plastic surgery is not dissimilar to tribal piercing or tattoos. I wouldn't begrudge many divas their fake eyelashes, hair extensions, self-tanners. Hell, I have some version of them myself: I have colored my hair, used tanning lotion and Latisse, an eyelash growth product. If I was going to see Cher, Dolly Parton, Britney Spears, game on. However, I would expect more passion, more emotion from them. If I was at a casino and Tori came out for a lounge act, I would have thought she lacked basic authenticity. Every toss of the hair, every embrace of the piano felt scripted.

Tori must have had her surgery at about my age (forty-four), which feels radically young. It's complex for women. One of the most authentic women I know had breast augmentation and so did one of the shallowest. If Tori wanted to wow us she could have written songs about being a woman about to turn fifty. Halfway through the show I said, "Rain, never get your skin resurfaced" (she is self-conscious about acne scars) to which she replied, "And you never get hair extensions" (I am self-conscious about my Tori-like hair).

I can't help comparing her to two other performers I saw at the same locale, one being Sting. Here's the scorecard: Wrinkles? Yes for Sting, no for Tori. Singing the same old hits from twenty years ago? Yes for both of them. Connecting with the audience, working the edge, being authentic, only Sting gets a check on that one. The other was Joan Baez, who was, like Sting, beautifully gray and wrinkled. With the latter two, the audience felt connected, that their songs of heartache and their creative struggles were relatable. Was it their lack of artifice? I can only assume so.

Facelifts so often create a mask, fine for the concert poster - in Tori's, plastered outside the Paramount, she looked like a Guinevere Barbie doll, airbrushed to perfection. Maybe that is why it is hard to find compassion or connection with overly-done faces, they seem devoid of emotion. I feel cheated and assume no one is home, that the inner workings are also nipped and tucked. Plastic perfection has never been the path Rain or I were interested in. This concert was a resounding echo to that impulse - give us runs in the stockings, give us a tired-looking soul singer who needs a better bra, give us wrinkles and strands of gray hair.

At the end of Tori's concert was a weak encore, both given and received. Rain and I were happy to leave. Anticipating meeting back up with Kristin and her dad, I hissed, "Don't say a thing about how we did or did not like it." Even though Kristin can fully join our ironic humor, she has an innocence I did not want to tarnish. I had a feeling Rain and I, being the Sagittarians (negative qualities include being overly critical, tactless, outspoken) were the only haters.

On cue, Kristin and her dad arrived breathless:

"Oh, wasn't it amazing, the way she worked the bench between the piano and keyboard?" they said in unison.
"Oh, to be that piano bench," her pop mused.
"Didn't you love her outfit?! Wasn't her voice incredible?!" Kristin concluded.

Yes and yes and yes. I could feel Rain, like I, reveling in our little Aquarian's (generous, thoughtful, idealistic) joy as we said our farewells.

I feel sadness for Tori. Here is a woman who for most of her career, challenged societal expectations of women head on, discussing sexuality, religion, masturbation, relationship, rape. Tori shared with us the secrets of her heart, embraced very difficult subjects and turned them into art. Here at this last juncture however, on how to be a powerful, passionate woman at every age, she fell silent.

On Why Not To Wear a Wig Onstage
by Rain

 Because prettier and neater
isn't better

Because fake, false movement
cannot replace real

Because perfect is never
interesting

On why not to get a face lift

Because tighter and smoother
isn't prettier

Because one surprised expression
cannot replace
the shifting myriad of emotions
that used to cross your face
that used to inform your work
that used to tell us

a soul resides here.

Carry On Wayward Son
by Deborah

My sixteen-year-old son, Misha, and I were redecorating the bedroom that his big brother had vacated to go to college. Gone were the hippy tapestries on the wall and the hippy-er posters. The avocado green paint was next. My boys love each other very much, but have always had a very different aesthetic. The younger of the two is clean-cut, preferring Nike logos to peace signs. It was fun to give him some attention, to go to the hardware store to pick out paint. He chose Ralph Lauren Ripstop Blue, a bold saturated color I argued would be way too dark.

Misha is Type A, likes to make decisions quickly. He also has great instincts. One half wall in, I agreed with his choice, genius really. Misha got his iPod out and asked if I wanted to hear "this cool song." With the first familiar bars, I recognized the classic, "Carry On Wayward Son" by Kansas.

I had to laugh when he asked me if I had heard it, as it was the very stuff of my high school years, when I was almost the same age as him. He played Journey's "Don't Stop Believing" next. Those early rock bands weren't my favorite, I preferred so-called new wave music, but I have since, thirty years later, gained much appreciation for several aspects - the harmonies, the musicianship, the bands' longevity, their often humble roots.

"Wayward Son" was written by Kansas guitarist, Kerry Livgren. According to Livgren, it was not written to express anything specifically religious, though it certainly expresses spiritual searching and other ideas. People have attributed all sorts of alternative meanings to it, but he suggests taking the song as it is. Listening to "Wayward Son" with my son was quite different than trying to dance to it at the junior prom. I heard it anew - this time "son" felt relative. My son isn't wayward, but the song reminded me of moments I thought my boys were veering slightly off course and how our children's paths are not our own.

Misha then put on some rap by a Somalian named Kanaan, a man who has seen more violence as a boy than any human ever should, who turned wayward with revenge, but ultimately healed his trauma through his music. Macklemore was next, a Seattle rapper who hit number one on the iTunes charts with a fun song called "Thrift Shop." Macklemore is a performer all my older children and I have been following, appreciating that he turned his addictions into art with the song "Otherside" and supporting same-sex marriage with "Same Love."

About halfway through our renovation, Misha petered out, laid prone on his bed and watched me paint the trim. I was happy to let him DJ. At the end of the afternoon, we had what felt like a brand-new bedroom and a strengthened connection, carrying on together with music.

A Babysitter Who Could Belt it Out
by Kristin

Recently I hung out with Rain and her main squeeze, chatting away, a bottle of wine between the three of us. It was delicious to talk, laugh and be totally absorbed in musical musings. I brought along chanting by Mitchell Gaynor (renowned for his singing bowl tones), music that brings comfort to those with diseases like cancer and AIDS. These healing sounds are a direction I would like to see Violet move into.

Feeling in the zone after our wine, we headed out for an evening in Olympia. I had heard an all-girl band was performing, but did not remember the name of the club they were playing at. We started at one of our favorite haunts, Cryptatropa, "The Vampire Bar" as Rain calls it, where revelers are greeted by a giant statue of a goblin. It is a thrill to walk in and absorb the energy, pure darkness in hue, but all I could feel was the light. No music though, darn. Off we went.

We decided on Le Voyeur, a restaurant and bar with a performance space the size of a shoebox where outrageous expression is always on the menu. In the past, Le Voyeur has not been somewhere that I have felt comfortable as it had triggered the shadow parts of my psyche. But I have since learned how to zip myself up energetically and not take on others' feelings. This is progress, as I have struggled my whole life with being a "sensitive."

Prior to tonight, we Violets have witnessed a transexual in a white nightgown howling into the microphone expressing etheric beauty and primal urges. Not tonight. Instead, on stage was the band I had been searching for, Full Moon Radio. Even better, the lead singer was a woman named Allison who used to babysit my older son when he was two. When I saw her across the dimly-lit room, I couldn't help but yell, "Alli!" She shaded her face from the strong lights and asked, "Who's there?" We met face-to-face and hugged. I couldn't wait to hear her sing.

Sing she did. Her voice was gravelly and demanded the presence of each person in the audience. Luscious and loud. Intense and gorgeous. A completely different element than I am used to and I loved it. Bring it on!

A sweet little cutie from Minnesota grabbed my arm and pulled me up front with her to dance. Rain joined us and soon we were sweating, jumping and cheering. This band had electric and bass guitars, a lead vocalist and a drummer (who Rain thought was primo). Seeing this young woman who used to wipe my son's nose fully embody her dream gave me inspiration to keep working on Violet's own unique style.

Giddy Up Let's Go
by Deborah

The morning of my birthday, my boyfriend asked me what I wanted to do. I said, "I don't care as long as we hang out *and* we have sex." There is a book called the *Five Love Languages* by Gary Chapman and mine are quality time and touch, in that order (the others being acts of service, spoken words of love and gifts). We had recently enjoyed Sting at the Paramount Theatre as a joint birthday adventure, so I was feeling satiated in the quality and time department. Touch, and a certain kind, was my top priority.

Earlier in the day, my daughter reminded me of her evening middle school choir concert. Remembering the last one, which lasted only a half hour, I didn't worry about missing out on a mini-date with my man. He was happy to go. We snuggled in the auditorium and glanced at the program while we waited for my girl to come on stage. This time, unfortunately, the seventh and eighth grade bands were playing as well.

The singers were sweet as could be, they sounded great - in fact, as good as the fancy private choir we used to pay fifty dollars a month for. Karina's choir teacher is a kick: she dresses up in black glitter and looks like a forty-year-old Scarlett Johansson. She, unlike me, is one of those people who looks beautiful singing. I love how she gesticulates to keep the kids' attention, could watch her all night.

Well, almost all night. I was feeling antsy, knowing my birthday window was closing. BF and I were both sleep deprived and I knew after eleven we would be worthless. I could barely sit still as we watched the arduous transition from choir to band, seemed it was the one piece that hadn't been rehearsed. Music stands and chairs had to be arranged, bleachers and the piano pushed back. Five minutes stretched to ten, and not being a big band person, I wasn't excited about the next gig anyway. Without lyrics, I am often bored.

From the first tuning, however, my curiosity was piqued. I had never been this close to eighty musicians before. They played some folkish holiday songs with finesse and then moved on to more traditional tunes, most notably, a sing along. My boyfriend and I joined in, our mouths an inch or so apart. My guy has the best speaking, laughing, *hhmmming* voice; I would put it in the top five things I love about him. He does sing, but hams it up to the radio or while doing dishes and becomes self-conscious if I pay attention. This night I learned he also has a resonant singing voice! He can sing low! I took the soprano part and he, tenor. I'm sure we completely annoyed the people around us.

My honey was impressed by the conductor - from his tuxedo, complete with red cummerbund and matching bow tie, to the sharp wand he tapped in his hand, he meant business. He looked like an ex-marine: short hair, big muscles and an intimidating expression. I learned a few things, which always makes me happy. The whip sound is made by a percussion instrument called a "slapstick," just like it sounds. I am rather embarrassed to admit the next bit of information I gleaned by reading the printed lyrics to "White Christmas" which were in the program. My whole life I have thought "through the years we all will be together if the *fates* allow" was actually, "through the years we all will be together, if the *faiths* allow." Every time I heard that, I felt a wave of angst about the decisiveness of religion. A jolly nice feeling to let that go.

For their finale, the band played "Sleigh Ride." I loved the *clop, clop, clop* during the chorus, *giddy up, giddy up, giddy up let's go, let's look at the snow.* The snap of the whip thrilled me every time, especially later when my guy and I did get to celebrate my birthday and I was occasionally spanked with "Sleigh Ride" as a soundtrack!

ALL I WANT FOR CHRISTMAS IS NIRVANA
BY RAIN

Actually, I couldn't wait all the way until Christmas. My birthday falls two weeks earlier, and there on the breakfast table was the familiar flat, square-shaped present that announces: Look out! Mama's gonna get her rock star on.

This year marks the twentieth anniversary of Nirvana's hair-raising, ground-breaking *Nevermind*. The record that took "alternative," with all of its freaks and geeks, into the mainstream. That means I was already twenty-nine when "Smells Like Teen Spirit" took over the world. I was living in Spain at the time, far from the 1990's music-scene ground zero where I now reside. But when I look around at the Olympia men, the spirit of Kurt Cobain seems very much alive. In their plaid wool jackets, unwashed hair peeking out from under beanie caps, this area breeds a very specific type: a blend of artist and lumberjack, with a complex intellect and emotional terrain, choir boy cheeks, humble demeanor, a heart that sees suffering and longs to mitigate it, and a wild streak wide enough for salmon to spawn in.

When I visit Seattle and lose myself in the stream of hipsters in their self-conscious skinny jeans, cradling their non-fat Starbucks lattes, I miss those Oly boys. They won't be able to afford to buy you a beer after happy hour, they may not even have a room to ravish you in (or they may be too depressed to try), but their lively sense of irony should be enough to plug up those cracks in their Datsun windshields while they take you on the ride of your life. That green stuff on their teeth? Where do you think they got the term "grunge"?

VIOLET ROCKS!!! read the birthday card my girls made me, spelled out in purple ink, on the inside were the kind words:

We appreciate you so much! We love that you are doing what you love, starting your own band! You ROCK!

Their elation quickly waned as I dragged out a CD player and set it up on the kitchen counter. But I didn't care. I was Queen for the Day. I had considered asking for the Super Deluxe four CD/DVD, limited edition re-issue, but opted for ortho-donture for my younger child instead. This was all I needed, anyway - the original release, complete with a friendly photo of Kurt waving hello to us with his middle finger.

The iconic guitar riffs of "Teen Spirit" struck the air before the drums kicked it into the intricate, brutal, instantly recognizable Nirvana sound. The record has aged not one whiff. How is it possible for three people to throw themselves so completely into their work, without one false step? Touring must have honed their chops into this ninja-like daring. How could Kurt serve his guts up on a platter like that? One word describes their music for me: EXHILARATING. When I hear it again, I feel free, original, wise. What other songs were on here? Oh - "In Bloom"! "Lithium"! "Come As You Are"!

"Listen to this one," I exulted, as I cued up "Polly." I looked up briefly, to find my audience had discreetly melted away, probably to listen to Kesha or Rihanna from the safety of their ear buds. Oh, well. I didn't mind. In a way, I was reassured. *Alternative* was safely straddling the fringe once more, and I, Queen for the Day, was twenty-nine again! Hell, I might not even brush my teeth.

Buddy System
by Deborah

Just got back from having coffee with Kristin. She had asked for a Violet meeting, as she was at the bottom of a well, having had the flu last week, which left her depressed and edgy. We met at Sizizis, a coffee shop that feels like an enchantment with dark mahogany walls, and water served in heavy cut glasses. It seems your fairy godmother might stop in, wearing her velvet cape, having just distilled the tonic you need. We talked about the external contributing factors: her kids had been home for spring break, the endless gray days. We discussed Seasonal Affective Disorder and medication. Waiting in her medicine cabinet is a just-filled prescription of the antidepressant Zoloft, the little blue pills she poetically described as looking like buttercream mints.

As we spoke, Rain breezed in, she had just traded her peroxide mane for a sleek chestnut shag. We squealed at her new sophistication and then focused back on Kristin who had perked up some since I first arrived. Kristin has battled depression her whole adult life, perhaps mania as well. In addition to getting medical and psychological assessments, I urged her to make art of it, to jot down the steps that make her feel better, to be excruciatingly tender with herself. Sometimes, however, we can't even find our boots, let alone lift ourselves up by their straps. Sometimes that care is best offered by another, which is what Rain and I administered on a drizzly day, hoping like Simon and Garfunkel sang, to be the bridge over troubled water for our dear friend, who brings so much light to our lives, and yet finds herself engulfed too often in shadow.

Even though we are taught to team-lift heavy objects, in our individualistic society we are not coached to aid with heavy feelings and experiences. I remember a dishtowel my grandmother embroidered with, *If all of our troubles were hung on a line, you would take yours and I would take mine.* I never liked that, even though I understood inherently that we can't save someone else, I preferred the image of two women folding clothes together while laughing and crying, sharing burdens.

Sitting with Kristin, I flashed on when I took scuba diving lessons. I was impressed that each air tank was equipped with a second regulator, the breathing apparatus that delivers oxygen. Fewer places than underwater is the buddy system more critical. I loved learning the universal signals so we could communicate without words underwater:

not ok, danger, I am cold, out of air, something's not right, watch me, you lead and I follow.

If only on land, we could have such clear SOS symbols of need. With Violet, we seem to have an uncanny sense of taking up the slack. With practical matters such as editing, or working on our website, at least one, and most of the time, two of us have stayed on course. More importantly, as friends, we have taken turns propping each other up, we have never all fallen at once. I have the image of the fireman's carry, of two of us linking our arms for support, while the other may recover, being carried along.

Nutcracker, Nutcracker, Crack Me a Nut
by Rain

We all sat around the Happy Teriyaki table, three moms dressed like penguins and five girls in false eyelashes, mouse whiskers, shellacked buns and sweatpants. We didn't draw a single stare. Everyone within a mile radius of the Johansen Olympia Dance Center knew: it was Nutcracker season!

We had an hour between shows to grab a bite to eat. Two hundred ballerinas and their families descended upon the town like a plague of elegant locusts, ready to devour anything not nailed down. Our tuxedo-y outfits (black bottoms, white tops) were for ushering that night's show. Every family is required to volunteer four times during the two-week run. I have sold flowers, sewn sequined appliques onto tutus, and painted faces in the decidedly unglamorous bowels of backstage, which smells mostly of sour feet.

This is my daughters' sixth Nutcracker. They have progressed from mouse to party girl to Russian to snowflake. This year, my older daughter has her first lead part. It's over in a three-minute blur of white petticoats and red bric-a-brac, but in her heart, it will remain a high-water mark for much, much longer.

Last summer, it looked unlikely that the girls would be able to continue their dance studies. As a newly single mother, food on the table and a reliable car were my most pressing concerns. Ballet quickly became a luxury. Except I knew that it really wasn't, given divorce, re-location, new schools. These girls had

had enough change and challenge. One thing needed to remain constant for them to love.

For my daughters - performers to the bone, and kinesthetic learners to boot - dance is an inherent part of their beings. *Ballet is Work*, reads the Harvey Edwards poster of a man, face contorted in concentration, stretching at the barre. Work that requires years of dedication, discipline and drudgery to appear to float across the stage like a feather, defying gravity and everything else that threatens to weigh down the spirit that longs to soar.

I appealed to my family for help, and they rallied. My parents and siblings agreed to split the cost between them for the upcoming year. My father wrote a supportive note. "I'm thrilled the girls are being exposed to Tchaikovsky's brilliant score," he shared. I was reminded of, and grateful for, all of the music that had poured out of his two-foot high speakers in every house we ever lived in. If I think of Chopin as the thinking girl's sex symbol, it's surely due to my father's influence. Not only classical, but jazz, bossa nova, and even the Beatles and the Who. By watching him lose himself for hours in record after record, I learned to give myself over to the experience thoroughly and completely. As we chowed down our chow mein, eager to descend the concrete stairs to the dressing rooms again, I was moved to see the next generation of my family reveling in the musical world.

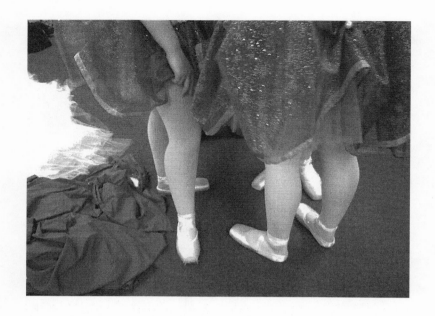

What Would Violet Do?
by Deborah

Violet has become a persona in her own right.

In the area of fashion, she absolutely is consulted. Rain recently texted me a picture of a pair of fabulous boots and asked if she was too old for them, I asked simply, *What would Violet buy?* Duh, the boots instantly became a no-think.

Beyond the superficial fashionista, however, we are finding that Violet is the more confidant, carefree, gamine, glamorous woman we always hoped to be. She is full of love and sparkle. She is our highest, best self.

Anais Nin wrote that we all need to create our own mythology. Jean Houston, a scholar who was pivotal in founding the human potential movement and studied mythology with Joseph Campbell (author of *Hero With a Thousand Faces*), states on her website that:

> *Those of us who work with myths... and have entered the realm of the ancient stories and their personae, seem to inherit a cache of experience that illumines and fortifies their own. They soon discover that they too are valuable characters in the drama of the world soul, pushing the boundaries of their own local story and gaining the courage to be and do so much more.*

What we ladies found as we assessed our lives before this adventure, was a multi-layered yearning for magic, mystery, fun, community and focus. Hanging out with our peers, we find many are drained, depleted and depressed. We find women (and men) who have abandoned their aspirations or never even thought to have them in the first place.

In some ways, we could have chosen anything. Running a marathon, joining the PTA, taking up horseback riding may have sufficed to give the jolts of passion, inspiration and connection we were looking for. We knew we needed something out of the box, something a little on the edge and something we deeply cared about.

Spiritual gurus suggest that the reason we do anything is to feel happy. *Just get happy first!* they cheer, offering the two main tools - being in the present moment and feeling gratitude for exactly where you are at. I agree these attitudes should be bedrock, but also know many of my greatest joys are from working at something and achieving it. I feel very blissed out on top of a mountain looking at the beauty below me, but I am on top of the world happier having learned to snowboard, feeling like a dolphin riding the surf making my way down. I like listening to a singer, but gain greater satisfaction learning the song and re-interpreting it. We humans are both be-ers and do-ers; this creative impulse is what separates us from the animals.

Having this framework, this mythological character larger than the three of us, Violet, has allowed us to adopt a *fake it until you make it* attitude. We are almost daily surprised how others have bought right in. "How is the band?" I am asked in the first few minutes of most conversations with friends. The truth sometimes is, "Wow, we haven't done much musically." But we have kept dreaming. Rain and I have consistently met for over two years once a week and spoken of our vision. Kristin has joined in physically during most of this journey, emotionally, one hundred percent.

When we sabotage ourselves, believing we are too old, unskilled or everyday to be worth our creative attention, Violet waits patiently, knowing otherwise.

What Is My Gift, Anyway?
by Kristin

I had a few songs that I needed to memorize the lyrics to. To many this would be a no-brainer, but it is actually very difficult for me. I can remember some things so easily, like people's names, for instance, and their kids' names, but a song? Oh God, I struggle. Then when I throw guitar chords in, I am almost unable to keep up. Even though I have had success with the song, "Can't Let Go," a few months ago, I still am challenged.

I have pondered this fear and keep coming back to the fact that routine recitation has never held any appeal for me, even as a child. In school, I worked very hard to deal with ADD and as a young adult, I gravitated toward playing with children, cleaning houses, dancing to my own rhythm - nothing that required any rote learning, whatsoever. So what to do when others are counting on me to perform?

I have already tried two instruments and still feel the same way. Although I know all beginners go through a learning curve, I am afraid there is more to it than not wanting to put in the time. Making new brain connections takes presence and commitment. I find no joy in practicing the same song over and over and am afraid even if I did, this goal just might not be possible.

I was sharing this with the band when Deborah offered some insight and relief. She told me that my gift is *ecstatic expression in the present moment.*

It's true. I remember at our first performance when the keyboard went out and I grabbed the shaker next to me and started dancing joyfully, I felt most comfortable. And I did inspire, as Deborah keeps telling me, Mark from Rhythm Fire has mentioned several times, that he will never forget how fun I was to watch. Letting go of having to play instruments in a traditional way, I feel as though I have been given a huge gift and a hall pass at the same time. I want to be able to perform with Violet and am so relieved Deborah has suggested that to do that, I let go of any preconceived expectations and do what comes naturally.

The Visual Violet
by Deborah

Recently, Rain arrived for our monthly sleepover with her customary cloth bag under one arm (drumsticks poking out) and an artist's portfolio under the other. She brought us into the music room, cleared the amp wires from the center of the floor, untied a black ribbon on the folder and ceremoniously laid out several collage masterpieces, one more compelling than the next.

In each, Rain surrounded a central figure with symbols from nature and culture, completed with a printed action word as a guide. Among her first creations, were *Submerge, Grieve, Question,* and *Manifest.* Her palette consists of magazine images which she sculpts and schmoozes, creating powerful stories on paper. Pablo Picasso and Max Ernst, who dabbled in this art form, would have been sharpening her scissors.

We had long spoken of making "cards," as we girls have always enjoyed using classic tarot, dream, angel, and manifestation decks. We often lament the dated art work and uninspiring graphics, longing for fresh and hip images that fit our modern lives. Rain's beauties immediately filled the gap. Violet Vision Cards, she's calling them.

Her goal is to spice up her nannying job by making one inspiration card a week. With little ones afoot it is impossible to form a coherent thought, yet alone steal a moment on the computer for writing, so she is choosing this school-age craft form, cutting images and gluing them on paper, elevating it to a high art. The little girls she tutelages *ohhh* and *ahhh* over the pretty colors and feminine shapes, and make their own versions alongside her - Maria Montessori would have been proud (she asserted children do not want to merely play, but crave practicing the tasks and skills of adults). Rain can assemble in spurts - cutting out a bird, then cutting up a banana for a toddler, gluing a vibrant violet border, then administering a kiss.

Some pursuits take single-pointed focus; writing and practicing music are among them. Some can be visited and re-visited, the time in between allowing the images to float and later find their natural place. It is a nice balance to have these complementary processes. Rain has been nose to the grindstone, finishing her pieces for our book and her memoir, *To the Moonhut,* about the period following her divorce. Now it is time to play, a copy of *Vogue* magazine and a travel brochure in hand. Rain is inspiring us once again, taking Violet in a new direction to include visual delights, opening up the possibilities for our offerings, following her muse, with her lavender taffeta swish.

New Year's Resolve
by Deborah

Two days into the new year, we Violets had a stunted version of a Band Retreat. Kristin had been epic in planning a Portland RV jam, where we would have soaked in hot springs for a weekend. Problem was the only thing I could show up for was my kids. The rest I left open for snowboarding with my man this time of year. Rain was similarly non-committal.

We settled on meeting around my kitchen table. Kristin arrived on fire. She had a box of goodies: an altar on the go containing candles, essential oils, journals and art magazines to share. She regaled us with stories of how she rocked a dance party out there in little ol' Union (she was sore for three days). Rain and I listened to her adventures and her vision for our band. We were happy to tack the sails, while we watched her steer our Violet ship into the wide open sea.

Very New Years-y like, we made a goal to each have thirty written pieces completed by June when we would begin to edit our work and see if we had learned as much as we thought we had, if it would be inspiring to others and if we could make a memoir out of our journey. We also set our sights on performing not on a stage, but a street corner. Anywhere.

Each of us have our own personal timelines and goals around this larger-than-life entity we have so lovingly created. I cannot decide if I should sing with Mark or not. I love it when I am there with him, but once I am home alone, I really enjoy the groove I get into with my own music. I feel I would do well to get the songs under my belt that I have already been working on. Money is definitely an issue. My oldest son is in his first year of college and my divorce is final in three months. The pie will be a bit smaller, and cut into more pieces. Our studio time with Skyler is not efficient because Rain and I don't practice enough together and I don't solidly know the songs. I am also the one with the most time on my hands. No excuses.

I have committed to learning guitar, for myself and Violet. I have a playlist of a dozen songs I would like to have the chords and lyrics memorized to, an expansion of what Mark and I performed last spring. I am not even worried about intros (or exits!), bridges or solos, just the bare bones, what any beginning guitar book would have its students accomplish. I am embarrassed to say after a year and a half of imagining and holding the vision of Violet, I am still at this place.

My Pregnancy
by Kristin

Recently my husband and I became pregnant with our third child. I was on the fence about having another baby. Part of me was in love with the idea of having a little one to caress again and babies give me a much desired sense of purpose. The other part of me was filled with dread.

Currently, even though I have moments of strife, I have a wonderful rhythm with my kids. My younger son, Azure, is about to enroll in kindergarten and my older boy, Coletrane is approaching the second grade. I am just entering the sweet spot. Coletrane is outgoing and loves to imitate my dancing. There is no doubt we are meant to butt heads and learn a great deal about ourselves through each other. Azure still climbs all over me every day and is endlessly supplying me with flowers he picked and dozens of kisses.

Next year will be the first time they are both in school. Already, a neighbor has begun to watch the kids at her house while I get some writing in. This is new. For the first time in years, I have more ME time, getting out of the house regularly. Starting over again with a newborn, ultimately means spending another seven years close to home. Nonetheless, despite some ambivalence, deep stirrings couldn't be ignored and I opened to this pregnancy.

My thoughts soon drifted beyond my family, to how it would work for me to breastfeed-on-demand, learn a new instrument and perform at gigs. Scared to shatter our dreams, I was more than hesitant to let Rain and Deborah know of my new path. Was I alone messing up the plan? Would they be disappointed in me? Six months prior, I had already taken a leave of absence from Violet. What gave me solace was visualizing laughing with them on Deborah's bed at our next Violet band meeting. I imagined us dancing a jig after my announcement.

The girls did a jig and more - they assured me having a baby was as much a part of my path as Violet and promised it would all work out. Something still wasn't right in the pit of my stomach though, even after I embraced my pregnancy. I got still and felt what I was really scared to face, that having a baby at this junction in my life would cause me to stay home and avoid the next phase of my life.

I was also afraid of my experiences mothering very young children in the past. While raising Coletrane and Azure, I was deeply depressed, constantly roaming the dungeons of my mind. My house became dirty, I didn't shower and cancelled plans with people at the last minute. I became anxious and alone. I couldn't deal with the down time as a stay-at-home mom. Instead of coping with my circumstances by finding play groups or child care so I could get out of the house and work part-time, instead of doing spiritual work on the origin of my fear, I used sugar and other stimulants to numb the pain. Sugar momentarily opened the portal to bliss. I ate sweets when I could not access the sweetness in my life. But, when the euphoria wore off, I became upset, having meltdowns more often than my young sons. I targeted my anger toward my husband, almost ending my marriage.

During both pregnancies and as a new mother, I dwelt in a constant state of mania: in one moment, harmonious and present to the boys' needs, playing with abandon; in the next, eating, raging and suffering. Joining Violet was the anchor that I craved. Being in the joyful company of Rain and Deborah lifted me out of my malaise.

My love for my growing family was truer than my mood swings, but as the pregnancy weeks went on, fear and resentment took root. Still, I tried to hold onto the light, onto the part of me that wanted to be a mother again. I have had very difficult pregnancies in the past and I tried to make this one different. I told the babe that I loved him/her and thanked them for being my teacher. I was making strides, with the help of my supportive husband, I was able to handle the depression and extreme nausea. When I felt like I could not get out of bed, he put his hands on my belly and did Reiki. He reminded me to feel, rather than medicate.

I tried to look at the depression as a sensation rather than a perpetual state of mind. Using creative visualization, body work and sound therapy, I felt a renewed sense of hope and stability, ready to have this pregnancy, most likely my last, be a divine, different experience. However, it was not to be. My miscarriage happened four days later.

Tell All or Tell Small?
by Deborah

Rain, Kristin and I wonder how much back story (and front story!) to include with Violet. The musical journey is a plateful; we could easily write about it alone without touching on our "real" lives. We argue that music is revealing anyway: making certain sounds, listening to certain music illuminates plenty. All three of us enjoy leaving our personal baggage at the door and focusing on something other than children and men for a few precious hours a week. Our intention with the band and the band memoir is to explore music - the creation that carry us up and beyond, that heals and holds us while we cobble together our emerging lives.

Self-esteem is a slippery thing and all three of us Violets, in focusing on our children, have not achieved what other women have in terms of career goals. It is one thing to pat yourself on the back when your kids are doing well, but what about when they are not? Or grow up and away? You cannot look at a child, whose life is out of your hands in large part, the same way you look at a published book or a spreadsheet. They do not give you the feedback a client or patient might. And while we don't believe how we feel about ourselves should be based on what we do, at the end of the day, attainment does partially define us. This theme, how to balance our personal lives with our creative longings, surfaces again and again.

We are at a crossroads. We began Violet, in part, to sow our post-divorce, post-thirties and forties wild oats. But a desire to express deeper experiences was born. Thus our vision as a band has emerged from us wanting to be on a stage and have men throw their boxers (or briefs!) at us, to hosting debaucherous middle-aged dance parties, to finally, cuddling up on Friday night to practice our harmonies. All the while, our very wooly lives have been tumbling along: divorce papers have been signed, children have adjusted, new relationships have begun and a flailing marriage rekindled.

In some ways, we would like to be granted the same carte blanche for art that has been given men in any artistic endeavor. Keith Richards is not asked about his children or rehabs during interviews, no one seems to notice or care Rod Stewart is on his fourth wife. Most men are granted a certain amnesty regarding their personal and family life and even more license to create in general. However, women tend to be mothers and wives first, juggling our passions with equal measures of desire and guilt. We wonder how any given performer/writer/artist produces with families in tow, as we find we are often not managing more than the fires that flare all around us.

When there is major life transition such as a separation or divorce, or even turmoil within a marriage, when a new child is added to the mix, the seismic plates shift for everyone involved. Among just we three, we have experienced depression, financial woes, injuries, a dash of SAD (SDD or Seasonal Defective Disorder we prefer to call it), a major birthday ("Turning fifty anyone?"). And it is not only the challenges, a new school routine can throw us, even a novel hobby such as my snowboarding diverted me. It is no wonder two years after we birthed Violet, she is still a fledgling.

One of the main lessons we have learned, is that monumental fortitude is required to rise above the muck and actualize *anything*. We have scaled back, started smaller and started again. We decided to tell almost all because it is our emotional and physical backdrop (especially when we give our attention solely to our kids and colds and break ups and breakdowns) that so easily keeps us from doing what we desire. We feel embraced and bolstered when we read memoirs by women like Erica Jong, Eve Ensler and Julia Cameron, who juggle outer and inner work, sharing their struggles and strengths, inspiring all the way.

What My Unborn Baby Gave Me
by Kristin

I woke up feeling out-of-sorts, but went to take a hot shower, as it seemed to help with my morning sickness and generalized feeling of panic. My sons wanted to join, paying close attention to my belly, excited that a new baby brother or sister was growing inside me. They loved to tell it stories about what great brothers they would both be. They promised to start helping out with the chores, as I had told them this baby was going to demand a lot of my attention. My youngest, Azure, was set on having another boy whereas his big brother, Coletrane, wanted a sister because he wanted me to have someone in the family who could understand my girly ways and who reminded him of me.

As I was drying my leg, a large bubble of blood dropped to the floor, stark against the white tile. It reminded me of the first time I got my period in gym class in the eighth grade. Cole stared at it for a moment before exclaiming, "Mama, what is happening?" I knew immediately that our baby was making an exit. I felt conflicted because I wanted this baby and yet it was the first time in weeks that I did not feel nausea or extreme depression. I could feel immediately my hormones balancing, bringing a sense of calm. That moment cemented for me that all was as it should be.

I told Cole that I was unsure of what my body was doing, even though it seemed clear. I laid down in our bed with a towel underneath me. I bled a little more, remembering that sometimes women spot during pregnancy, anxious to see what would happen over the next hour. While I ate lunch, I could feel myself starting to bleed again. I went to the health clinic and they told me that I needed to go to the hospital to have my miscarriage.

I did not heed their advice, but instead dropped off my sons at a caregiver and then went to a dear friend's so that she could tend to me, as my husband could not leave his post at the busy restaurant he managed. I did not expect to be in such pain, but my uterus was strongly contracting. It felt like I was birthing, rather than expelling the fetus of our unborn child. I alternated sitting on the toilet and in a warm tub. Unmedicated, after a few hours, I could hardly talk. I cried in anguish and then had periods of tranquility. I wanted my husband, who finally came and took me home. He placed his hands on my belly and did Reiki. I listened to a soothing whale song CD and feel asleep. I woke up feeling that I had undergone a metamorphosis.

Through the pain of miscarriage, I was able to truly find out how strong I am. I did not emotionally die with that baby, but felt *reborn*. I grieved over the coming months for the part of me that longed to give all of my attention to a newborn. I wanted a baby to need me so that I would not have to go out into the world.

I was quickly able to view the miscarriage from a different perspective; that the baby showed me that I could start giving attention to myself. I am dealing with my depression now, for the first time in twenty-five years. I am ready to embrace this time of my life. My sons are getting more independent, my husband and I are spending some quality time together while the kids are at school. Violet is starting to bloom and I feel stronger and healthier than ever. I am lavishing attention on myself, appreciative of the opportunity to see that I am worth every bit of love that I would have given that new baby.

I am back on an antidepressant. Coupled with an organic diet, daily yoga plus a whopping dose of Violet, I am conquering my melancholy. I am monitoring the sugar and stimulants and using better tools to manage my emotions. I am using Violet as a means to get myself out in the world, and finding it exciting rather than frightening. Motherhood is definitely one of my greatest accomplishments, however, it is not my only one.

Crowning
by Deborah

On a motivational tape, I once heard that *a time line is a dead line.* I nodded my head in agreement, feeling the inherent truth, that putting a linear end to the creative process kills the very thing one is after. And yet, yet, yet as I look at the material goods that surround me - the computer I type on, the bed, house, street, city I live in - most would not exist without expected endpoints. In most developing countries, it is the absence of reliable infrastructure that halts progress, the half-completed buildings, the lack of basic societal services are testaments to unmet goals of funding and focus.

This said, it is important to have flow in our lives. Somewhere. Violet has been an interesting balance for Kristin, Rain and I, to both fox trot and slow dance. With the music, we have been gentle as one would with a baby learning to walk, we have allowed our process, even though it has been excruciatingly slow to any bystander. We have pushed ourselves a bit more with the writing, setting an actual deadline for completion of this manuscript and our website.

The thing is, none of us wanted Violet to be a job-job. We wanted an experiment in serendipity, in intuition, in allowing, in MAGIC. We have enough of that other stuff in our lives, mostly centered around the schedules of our ever-active children: every parent knows the drill - soccer practice at four, ballet performance at six, college applications due next Friday, car needs oil change last month.

The term "crowning" is used to describe the point in the birth process when the baby's head is visible, often accompanied by a burning sensation called the "ring of fire," which feels like the vagina is being ripped open. Creative process often has a similar energy to it, psychically rather than physically, there is the feeling of carrying a project along, steadily nourishing it and then suddenly it is ready, it *has* to be birthed.

Violet has had the gestation of an elephant, about two years, alternatively moving in our bellies with slight murmurs, then kicking against our ribs with impatience. Lately we have all felt the contractions, a bearing down, something ready to be born. After going to the Snow Patrol concert and seeing Ed Sheeran perform "Wayfaring Stranger" a cappella, I told Rain and Kristin that we/I needed to move in a new direction. It was time to scrap the covers, lay down the instruments and find OUR sound.

With this realization, I stopped my music lessons completely. Shortly after, I picked up my phone, used the voice memo feature and recorded myself toning. I toned and moaned and groaned, moving from despair to ecstasy. I sang the spiritual, "I Went to the River to Pray." I then hummed it, and then sang single words: *No* and *Yes, Breathe* and *Open.*

As I got simpler, my voice became deeper, reaching a reservoir of feeling, opening a channel from my heels to the top of my head, a crown of light. This experience was then magnified and deepened at our next rehearsal, where we made our first authentic Violet sound. It took us two years and four wrong instruments and hundreds of dollars and dozens of lessons to get there. For this one place in our lives, we needed to not be bound by the linear world, to let the birth process proceed as the universe, not we, dictated.

Feelings, Nothing More Than Feelings
by Rain

We have been bashing away, off and on, at our instruments now for over two years. We've covered songs by the Beatles, the Pretenders, Lucinda Williams, and Fleetwood Mac. But our *own* style has proven elusive to uncover.

Being busy women with families has been something of a damper. Many bands go through an embryonic period where they share the same womb/apartment, and eat, sleep and breathe music together. The Beatles learned harmonies while literally piled upon each other in unheated vans to and from gigs. The Rolling Stones bunked up together early on, only leaving their Memphis-blues-filled flat to steal food. This sharing of everyday existence seems crucial in forging a band identity.

For a moment, I indulge myself in just such a fantasy.

It is four a.m., Deborah staggers over the spent body of her lover, emerging into the living room in one of her swishy mermaid skirts, her golden curls artfully tousled. She pops some salmon cakes in the oven, mixes up a pitcherful of Violet Vixens and joins Kristin and I around the fireplace, where we are hard at work on the chorus of our future breakthrough single. Me running my hands through my hair, as I do when inspired, and Kristin barefoot, her bass lovingly cradled in her lap. The glorious luxury of time, space, friendship, and a reeaally cool violet velvet settee. Oh, and - flattering lighting.

Then someone yells "MOM!" and I wake up.

On the other hand, busy women with families get very good at maximizing resources and multi-tasking. Deborah, Kristin and I check in with each other almost daily by texting, sending photos, quotes, or ideas that have us jazzed. "Forget red hats!" I burbled the other day, having just learned about the Red Hat ladies, middle-aged women who get together for social events wearing red hats (oh, and buying red note cards, and pins and boas and coasters - a merchandiser's dream). "We can offer violet tambourines and harmonicas to encourage everyone to play music. To hell with purchased entertainment! Make your own!"

We've also recently set aside every other Friday night as a band practice/sleepover night. Deborah throws together one of her abracadabra meals while the children (a baker's dozen) swirl around us: the young boys bouncing off the trampoline (or any other available surface), the older ones plotting at computers, the teenaged girls heading out to the mall or someone's school play. Then it's time for Violet to convene in the music room, a marvelous design with glass doors through which we can *see* the kids, but not hear them (or smell the blood).

And since the kids cannot hear *us*, either, we are now free to download the R-rated version of our past week to each other. Having touched base on all matters of the heart and its more southerly sister, our conversation drifts to music. We might share a YouTube video and discuss what it is about it specifically that moves us - ingenious simplicity being high on our list, like Gotye's "Somebody That I Used To Know."

Last week, Deborah had something new to share, and I could tell by her slight smile that it was something brave and maybe a little unnerving. I asked that the lights be turned low, which led to a candle being lit. "Shall we clear the space?" Deborah suggested. We lit a sprig of dried sage and blessed one another, wishing that all impediments to joy and light simply blow away. Then Deborah played us a recording she had made on her phone in, of all places, her minivan. On it, she hummed, she howled, she keened, she beat on the steering wheel. Her open-throated passion was mesmerizing. Kristin and I were riveted. Women in our society just don't let themselves loose to experience the full power of their voices very often.

"I thought we could try doing this," she continued. "Let's sit with our backs together, supporting one another." I grabbed an Irish drum, Kristin a shaker. It was amazing, feeling our backs and shoulders touching - the reverse of the hugs we always give each other. I started to beat the drum against the floor very slowly. I felt a little nervous, hoping the sounds that came out of me would be rich and round. *Toning*, Deborah had called it. It felt daring and soul-baring, and I was relieved to be among close friends.

Deborah started in first, with a sound that felt like *grief*. I focused on keeping the rhythm steady, like a heartbeat. I've noticed the calmer I am in my life, the steadier my drumming is. And I need to be steady - my band is depending on it. Kristin shook her rattle and added her full, resonant voice to the mix. A landscape opened up in my mind - an apricot sunset, a desert, a cool wind. I immersed myself in the setting and let a short howl escape me, then another longer one. It felt elemental, incredible. The mood and sounds switched to *excitement*, then *joy*.

I had recently begun making a series of collages based on emotions, or states of being, to be more exact, and this helped me access my feelings. *Reveal, Dare, Unleash, Devote, Transcend, Question, Frolic, Rage.* I have learned that feelings are like the weather, arriving and departing somewhat mysteriously (a blue day, out of the blue), but they are not *me*. I can choose to listen to and honor them, rather than stuffing or ignoring them.

Expression. Pure, simple, and authentic. A perfect place for Violet to start finding our own style. Perhaps vocalizing our emotions would help release them, and take away the temptation to foist them on our loved ones. Feelings, after all, are nothing to be afraid of, though many of us seem to spend our lives in a mad sprint to get away from them.

I had a dream the other night. The three of us were in a book-lined attic, all white and yellow. We stood in a circle and a ball of golden energy began to pass between our heart-spaces. *This is the real work of our lives,* I said. *Learning to work with this energy.* It felt out-of-this-world exhilarating. Ecstatic.

First True Sound
by Deborah

Kristin, Rain and I have been having Friday night pow wows at my house for a few months now. Both women bring their progeny and we ignore them while we talk a lot about and make a little music. This June first was my youngest's birthday and we double-dipped with a birthday cake and fanfare, let him think the fuss was all about him. After shooing the kids out of the music room, the girls and I got serious.

I brought down my phone with its voice memo-ed toning, a candle and sage. Rain showed us her latest collages which floored Kristin and I with their imagery, which is both powerful and playful. We took turns "smudging" one another and voicing our blessings. I then said a prayer for Violet:

Thank you creative spirit for our blessings,
for giving us a focus for our creativity,
for music in our lives and our hearts,
for the belief that we can make music ourselves.
We ask to be a light for others,
to share our gifts of positivity, of transformation,
of merriment and meaning.
We ask that our projects evolve in a way that is natural,
that they flow with ease and harmony,
that we are shown the way.

I played my demos. Kristin and Rain felt my authentic emotion, felt the opening I was able to achieve with my voice. We dimmed the lights and sat together, back to back. Rain grabbed a large Celtic hand drum and began tapping it on the floor in a rhythmic, heartbeat tempo, Kristin nabbed a shaker, seeds on a gourd.

I started toning very low, didgeridoo almost. Rain was the first to add true voice. Kristin and I joined in, and then the three of us created and rode the wave of our collective creation. Kristin shook the rattle at just the right time, Rain steadied us with a heartbeat tempo throughout. We took turns leading and following, calling and responding, there was no leader, no front woman. Rain, who for two years has been behind drums, who has been hesitant to sing harmonies, toned equally with Kristin and I.

I had done this kind of chanting before, but the girls hadn't. I hadn't done it exactly in this way, with just three, before it was always a kind of drum circle madness. This was extremely intimate, I could feel each of my beloved friends breathing against me. It felt holy.

After several minutes, we felt done; we were hot, sweaty, flushed. Was it music? Absolutely. We all want to continue on this track, seeing where this primordial beginning takes us. We realized we had leapfrogged over this seminal step, focusing on how we *should* play rather than what we wanted/needed to *say*.

This new direction, this authenticity was what we had been after all along. This was Violet.

Conclusion

This memoir concludes at a beginning. There is wisdom in knowing what you want, but also in knowing what you don't want. After two years of watching traditional bands set up shows at ten p.m. and party until three a.m., we know our journey will be a softer, sweeter road.

When asked, "How is the band?" the follow-up question is usually, "When is your next (first) gig?" Others want to experience us, especially with the two-year buildup! We find ourselves asking the same of fellow musicians. However, we have discovered we are not natural performers, rather we are natural writers and photographers and music lovers and bliss magnets and sparkle fairies.

We do love to sing and drum and strum, but conclude this chapter of Violet questioning whether the traditional look of a band, an audience-watching-performers, fits our essence. We keep coming back to how music, until very recent times, has been a community affair. We resource African drum circles, Native American chanting, Indian kirtan for inspiration and are most excited about inclusive experiences.

That said, we are as committed as ever to honing our craft - Deborah is finally willing to practice scales, Kristin has developed a trance dance yoga class and hints she might once again pick up the bass guitar, Rain is finishing the Violet Vision cards she collages and perfecting drum fills. We are as committed as ever to the idea of pulling back the curtain, of showing the in-between steps, so often missing in our perfection-driven, product-focused world. We are committed more than ever, because we are reaping the very real results of living and writing this memoir: Violet has strengthened our friendships and families, brought us joyful tears and hysterical laughter, and most importantly, instilled a sense of purpose and confidence gained only from having goals and bringing them to fruition.

At the time of this writing, we are putting the finishing touches to our new website, an upgrade from our original band-focused offering. We wanted a larger sandbox to play in than just Violet the band. This week on our collective Violet agenda: we are learning how to make electronic music with GarageBand; Deborah has her guitar lesson; Kristin is editing an interview with a street artist and Rain is working out harmonies for a song we want to sing a cappella. We continue to evolve, expanding our style, our voice, what we want to offer the world. We are honored you have shared our adventure. Please see us, hear us, join us in taking bitty and brazen steps at www.weareviolet.com.

About the Authors

Kristin, Deborah, Rain

Rain Cameron, Deborah Grace and Kristin Rizzieri, after ricocheting across the planet, found each other in Olympia, Washington. Despite broods of children and brimming schedules, they dusted off their turntables and vowed to reclaim the joy of their inner nine-year-olds at a slumber party, when they sang and danced as if anything was possible... because it is.

Please explore our website,

www.weareviolet.com

where we share regularly about our
music, meltdowns and muses.

Look for further Violet adventures in
2014, in our next memoir, "UltraViolet."

10418943R00165

Made in the USA
San Bernardino, CA
15 April 2014